$ 9.95 USD

*(For each copy sold, 10% will be donated to
The National Rifle Association to support them in their
endeavor to preserve gun-owner rights)*

This book is published in tribute to the National Rifle Association, who has been at the forefront of the effort to preserve gun owners' rights since its inception in 1871, and without whom it is questionable that private citizens in America would own guns today.

T&D
Publishing, LLC

Proudly published and printed in the USA

PRIVATE PACKERS

AN INTRODUCTION TO THE COMPLEXITIES
AND RESPONSIBILITIES ASSOCIATED WITH
THE CONCEALED CARRYING LIFESTYLE

Other books by this author

Novels:

"Above The Red"© 2013 ISBN 978-1-4817-6761-3
"Loweja"© 2013 ISBN 978-1-4817-6763-7
"A Certain Superstition"© 2013 ISBN 978-1-4817-6765-1
"A Parting Of The Clouds"© 2013 978-1-62994-687-0
"The Wolves Of Calamity"© 2013 ISBN 978-1-5301-3775-6
"Beyond Absolution"© 2014 ISBN 978-1-4897-0215-9
"Lang's Paradox"© 2016 ISBN 978-1-5300-6138-9
"Forever Will - From The Ashes Of War"© 2014
ISBN 978-1-4897-0343-9
"A Thousand Miles From Here"© 2014 ISBN in production
"Running The Distance"© 2016 ISBN 978-1-5300-6474-8
"Taylorstown"© 2015 ISBN in production
"Under The Influence"© 2015 ISBN in production
"Joseph"© 2016 ISBN 978-1-5238-8841-2
"Saddletramp" © 2016 ISBN 978-1530315451
"Stonemill"© 2016 ISBN 978-1-5300-9848-4
"Beyond The Sound Of Thunder"© 2016 ISBN 978-1-5350-59510
"The Sawtooth Cattle Company"© 2016 ISBN 978=1-5376-24440

Non-Fiction:

"Just Another Old Bowhunter"© 2009 ISBN 978-0-692-00281-0
"Another Old Bowhunter"© 2010 ISBN 978-1-4575-0977-3
"The American Feral Hog"© 2012 ISBN 978-1-4575-1405-0
"First Footsteps West"© 2013 ISBN in production
"Private Packers"© 2017 ISBN - 978-1-5428-5155-8

Table of Contents

Preface

Dr. David Landis

A while back, Tom told me that his intention in writing this book was to document the expression of his own personal feelings regarding the concealed carry lifestyle as well as offer some guidance to prospective concealed carriers and to "*stir the mental juices*" of those folks who have been concealed carriers for years. When I read his original manuscript, I felt as though he had accomplished just what he had set out to do, because his words had given me pause to consider my own personal status as a carrier of a concealed weapon. His words of caution contained in this treatise need to be heeded, read slowly, and reviewed closely before making a choice as to whether or not a person is going to become one of America's "*Private Packers*," as Tom puts it...

Concealed Carry is no lark! It is a deadly business...or, it can be. And as Tom so aptly illustrates in the pages herein, it is a business that must be taken very seriously by participants. We need to realize that it can also be a deadly business for a person to be in public places without the means of protecting themselves or their families.

When becoming a concealed carrier, one must be fully prepared mentally and physically, knowledgeable of their local laws, know the procedures to follow in the event that they are someday called upon to use their weapon in self-defense, and still be prepared for the eventual legal entanglements that can so often follow an event. Even when an armed individual is cleared of any misconduct or criminal issues... our civil laws often come into play when *"ambulance-chasing"* lawyers have an opportunity to convince a criminal's family that they have been wronged.

We see a lot of *"one-shot take-downs"* during the gunfights that are portrayed on television and in the movies.... Such is not usually the case in real life conflicts. Statistics, as well as surveillance video footage, has shown that many wounded assailants survive or continue to fight with single or even multiple gunshot wounds after they have been struck by a bullet, and especially when the bullet is one of a smaller caliber. Tom addresses that fact quite competently here in the pages that follow.

The cautions that we should be prepared and well trained with our individual weapons are not to fall on deaf ears! Perpetrators of violence have been known to comment that they would like nothing better than to take away a citizen's weapon and then turn it on them... The lesson for us is simple: Know how to use your gun as effectively as possible or don't carry one! Know the rules which should govern the behavior of a concealed carrier, or for everyone's sake, leave your weapon at home.

With good fortune and God's Grace, those of us in today's world who do choose to carry a concealed weapon will never have to use their firearm on another human being, but the old adage of "*better to be judged by 12 than carried by six*" may have compelling merit.

The highly visible liberals who get on camera and openly declare that American citizens do **NOT** need to own or carry firearms, are most often protected by a cadre of gun carrying protective service people... Interesting contradiction, isn't it?

The choice of whether or not we should arm ourselves is ours. If you live in a place where you're not allowed to make that choice, there is something wrong with where you live. Unarmed citizens are ***NOT*** citizens; they are "***subjects***" to the ruling body!

Go with God, and in peace, but make your own choices, carefully, thoughtfully and with full commitment to knowing and handling weapons of choice safely and effectively.

Forethought

The Second Amendment to the Constitution of the United States of America, conceived and penned by our forefathers in 1789, clearly states:

"A well-regulated Militia, being necessary to the security of a free State, the right of the people to keep and bear Arms, shall not be infringed."

On these grounds, for more than two hundred years, constitution-minded citizens have hereby exercised their right to bear arms without fear of these inalienable rights being sabotaged to any degree or in any manner by a dictatorial government. Recognizing the importance of our constitutional rights, our forefathers fought and died in order to grant us these and other rights, and so shall we fight and die if necessary in order to preserve them.

Politicians and special interest groups who have sought to abolish the Second Amendment, or change the wording in order to satisfy their own anti-gun agendas, have offered interpretations of the Second Amendment's *"true meaning"* as they see it – this, of course in an effort to effectively disarm the American people. If it wasn't such a serious issue, it would almost be humorous to listen to some of their arguments... arguments such as,

"Surely our forefathers didn't actually mean what they're saying here," or... *"If it was not for guns, there would be very little crime in America today,"* or... *"We have long surpassed any need for Americans to own guns and keep them in their homes,"* or... (my personal favorite) *"It was not our founders intention for these words to be taken literally."* Hmmm... Since when did our ingenious politicians become the mind-readers of our forefathers? And by what entitlement, other than dictatorship, would they take away our right to be armed?

A report issued in February, 1982 by a Senate Subcommittee that studied the Second Amendment published its conclusions, identifying and offering their opinion of the actual meaning and intent of the Second Amendment's wording by saying:

"The conclusion is thus inescapable, that the history, concept, and wording of the Second Amendment to the Constitution of the United States, as well as its interpretation by every major commentator and court in the first half-century after its ratification, indicates that what is protected is the individual right of a private citizen to own and carry firearms in a peaceful manner."

...and in a nutshell, that's a pretty accurate explanation of our Second Amendment right to bear arms, ...wouldn't you say?

Introduction

The overwhelming majority of level-minded people today would agree that guns do not commit crimes – people do. They would also be likely to agree that our constitution gives us the right to own guns, not only for sporting reasons, but also to keep them in our homes for the explicit purpose of defending our families. Where opinions often begin to differ, concerns the issue of our right to bear arms on our person when we are in the midst of other people, in public places. It's absurd to consider that we only have the right to defend ourselves when we're in our own homes (*the Castle Doctrine*), and all other times we should be willing to render ourselves at the complete mercy of anyone wishing to do us harm. Despite the many differences in opinion regarding an individual's Second Amendment rights to carry arms upon their person when in public, few people will fail to acknowledge the fact that the world we live in today is a much different place than it was thirty, or even twenty years ago. It's easy for gun-opposing liberals to condemn armed citizens as being something akin to pro-gun egomaniacs, but these same liberals who delight in bashing gun owners are to a great extent responsible for making the world we live in the dangerous environment that it is today. Consider for a moment the conservative peacefulness of the 1950's... the era of the post-war ultra-conservative... the era of *Ozzie and Harriet... Lucy and Ricky...* and *Leave It To Beaver...* It was an age in which family values were taught to younger generations, a time in which it was not necessary for us to lock our doors at night, and a time in which the keys were usually left in the ignitions of our family automobiles. (one automobile per family was the norm) It was also a time in which families regularly visited their places of worship – places where they could reaffirm their Christian values as a family unit and give thanks to God for their many blessings – blessings such as their sovereign security and safety.

For the most part, mothers and fathers were lovingly strict in the manner in which they raised their children – just as their parents had been stern yet loving disciplinarians before them, and they did not require the instructions of Dr. Benjamin Spock in order to know how to raise their children properly. The vast majority of moms and dads willingly accepted the parental responsibilities of teaching their children right from wrong, good from bad. Weekly allowances were not an entitlement, they were earned. By far, most American youngsters were taught at home to abide by the rules of society, to obey the golden rule, the Ten Commandments, and to cheerfully comply with Mom and Pop's edicts and instructions – **or else**. Mom and Dad's love went a long way in teaching their children right from wrong, but in the end analysis, within the young developing minds of our youth it was probably the "***or else***" that carried the most clout. Children were simply taught right from wrong in their own homes, and carried these concepts and principles into adulthood, abiding with them whenever they went into public. Sure, there were cases where heinous crimes were committed during the 1950's just as there have always been crimes in the world… ever since Cain decided to pick up a rock and slay his brother, Abel. But the scale of crimes committed during those years of peace and innocence, family sovereignty, and Christian values were miniscule and infrequent when compared to the crime statistics of today. What happened to us? How did we become a nation so inundated with crime? How did we become a nation that instead of helping their neighbors during a time of disaster, would take advantage of the situation by looting their neighbor's homes and stores? How did such deadly violence fester and migrate from the inner cities and find its way into the heartland of the nation's Bible belt? How did some of our children transform from being normal, harmless and innocently mischievous youngsters into the demented mass murderers who first conceived the heinous idea of bringing AK-47's into the classroom? The answers to these questions are debatable, subjective, and irrelevant at this particular point in time, because it is not the purpose of this book to bring sociological issues up for any type of open debate.

The fact that America's cities and towns have become a much more dangerous place to live than they were in past years is indisputable – it's a fact of life that each of us must live with, day in and day out. And yet those questions of how we got this way continue to haunt us. Will that innocent, all-American youngster who's sitting harmlessly in his or her room playing Nintendo today become the mass murderer of tomorrow's headlines? Will our very own community become the next scene of mass murder? If so, what can we do today to intervene, and prevent such a horrible eventuality... or at the very least minimize the number of potential victims? Even more important to us as heads of families, what can *I* do personally in order to increase the level of safety and protection for my loved ones as well as myself?

For those American citizens perceptive enough to see what's going on around them – those who refuse to ignore such issues and pretend that they or their families are immune to any type of threat, the basic need for self-protection has mandated that we get off our butts and take some sort of proactive measures – like obtaining the necessary skills and safeguards which might contribute someday to the safety and security of our families. The safety and well-being of our family is one of the most important primary obligations that each of us carry in life. Drastic and deplorable things continue to happen in the world around us every day – and prudence, along with good judgment, dictates that we should be aware of the fact that, God forbid, some day we could awaken to find ourselves or our families directly in the pathway of such indiscriminate and deadly conflict.

Actually, I don't consider this to be a book at all. I consider it to be more in the line of a treatise, a pamphlet, or a composition of recommendations.   Regardless, it is not my intention to make any attempts to unduly induce or encourage anyone into becoming a carrier of a concealed weapon. Recognition of the facts alone should be a sufficient motivating factor – with no need for scare tactics. Such a choice is something that each of us must make on our own, depending on our particular station in life, where we live, and our individual competency in the handling of firearms. Whatever choice we might make, we must also be prepared to live with the consequences. In the pages which follow, we will discuss some of the circumstances that contribute to the effectiveness of concealed carry, the awesome responsibility that comes with making such a choice, and some of the techniques which may hopefully assure us that we are in possession of the qualities, skills, and mindset which might enhance our efforts, making us safer, more capable, and more responsible armed citizens... and above all, more prepared for the unexpected as well as the unthinkable.

In the past decade and a half we have seen warped individuals committing crimes which were unimaginable during our earlier years of innocence. These terrible crimes have occurred in some locations which we have traditionally regarded as being, "*safe havens,*" or places where we would have least expected to encounter random armed violence or deadly encounters of any sort. Indiscriminate mass shootings have occurred in schools, college campuses, businesses, airports, shopping malls, and even in churches and synagogues.   And these locations have been chosen by the perpetrators – not by happenstance, but because the aggressors knew that they would be least likely to encounter armed resistance in these locations. The deviant cowards who plan and execute these types of crimes have no desire to confront any form of armed resistance, in fact, a skillfully armed public is their worst nightmare.

Innocent people and their children have lost their lives to the deranged whims of madmen whose wicked agenda seems to have been nothing but the senseless killing of as many innocent people as possible – killing purely for the sake of killing in order to exact some sort of revenge on society, make a bigger headline than their predecessors, or make some sort of mentally discordant statement so that the world will stand up and take notice of them. And if making a statement for the world to take notice is their motivation in perpetrating such crimes, our irresponsible and opinionated news media seems to always be more than happy to oblige.

Many politicians have reacted errantly to mass shootings by introducing legislation which superimposes a complexity of ineffective *'gun-control'* measures which only contributes to the further sterilization of our Second Amendment rights; as if such a foolish and illogical approach is going to serve as a deterrent to these criminal masterminds and assure society that something positive is being done – possibly enhancing their own political agendas and chances of re-election. Their tunnel vision in legislating new gun control laws is almost unbelievable, and has accomplished nothing more than the creation of meaningless, ineffective red tape as stumbling blocks for law abiding Americans wishing to purchase a firearm.   And all the while that these nearsighted politicians are at work trying to erode and eliminate the Second Amendment to our Constitution, attorneys and lobbyists for organizations such as the National Rifle Association and other pro-gun alliances are working equally as hard to defend and preserve a private citizen's right to own and bear arms. Meanwhile, the law-abiding, gun-owning citizen is caught somewhere in the middle – and such is the state of the world we live in today. Liberals continue to categorize our rights to bear arms as it relates to concealed carry, as some sort of legalization which permits gun-toting terrorist cowboys to flourish among our society... ready to draw their weapons at the slightest provocation and start blasting away at whatever may irk them – just like the maniacs who commit mass murders for no justifiable reason at all. To these misguided liberals and politicians, everyone who owns a gun must surely have the same wicked agenda.   Thankfully, statistics collected by impartial government sources have shown that such a thing is far from the truth. (*see page 25*)

Come with me in the pages which follow. In the most prolific and basic sense, the practice of concealed carry is a unique mindset as well as a lifestyle which proclaims that, "*If I or my family are at risk of becoming a victim of violent crime, I will not stand idly by and allow it to happen without presenting the most effective means of resistance possible and within my capabilities."* If you are considering the possibility of becoming a concealed carrier during all or part of the time you and your family spend in public places, or merely considering the purchase of your first handgun for the protection of your home, the following chapters may assist you in making some of the many important decisions which you will be facing. If you are a veteran in the field of gun ownership and concealed carry, why not take this opportunity to refresh yourself on the many aspects and responsibilities associated with being armed in public? The popularity of the concealed carry lifestyle has spawned a variety of options available today that were not available in years past, such as a sundry of new firearms which have been engineered and designed specifically with concealed carry in mind. Together, we'll take a closer look at some of these options as well as some of the different types of firearms. We'll also discuss some of the safety concerns of having a home-protection firearm in your house, and the most effective means of keeping that firearm secured and away from the curious hands of children.

Responsible gun ownership – An American Heritage and an American Right

A Few Eye-Opening Facts
Pertaining To The Practice Of Carrying Concealed Weapons

It should come as no surprise that the number of citizens finding it advisable to carry a defensive weapon on their person during the time they spend outside their home, when they are in public places, has increased dramatically in recent years. There had been a gradual increase across America during the decades leading up to the twenty-first century, but in the eight years which followed the election of our nation's forty-fourth President, the numbers have absolutely skyrocketed – for reasons which are perfectly obvious. Our forty-fourth President made no attempt to hide the fact that he was an avid anti-gun President, who would have been delighted if he had been successful in completely abolishing the Second Amendment and disarming America altogether. His vigorous anti-gun enthusiasm created a mild panic among responsible gun owners, and his narrow-mindedness as our Commander-in-Chief sparked a sale of firearms and ammunition across the country which had never before been equaled in America. In some instances, firearm manufacturers worked their factory employees around the clock in a futile attempt to keep up with the increased demand, and even then could only satisfy about a third of the orders which poured in for new guns and ammunition on a timely basis. And even when the initial demand for firearms had peaked, the orders did not subside, they kept pouring in. In President Obama's eagerness to disarm America he had created a surge in firearm sales which had been unprecedented in the history of our country. Citizens who had previously never had a desire to own the more '*combat-oriented*' or tactical weapons such as the AR-15, or an AK-47, rushed to their gun stores in order to purchase one before they might have been banned altogether. Gun dealers had their shelves stripped of ammunition as citizens sought to stockpile supplies while they could. In the President and the Secretary of State's verbal attacks on gun-owner rights, they had inadvertently created a boon in gun sales and gun ownership unparalleled in the history of our country. (*Thank you Mr. President*)

Motivated purely by a desire to adequately arm themselves for reasons of personal defense, citizens by the millions began to take action in procuring additional firearms and ammunition – driven by the overwhelming desire to have a more effective means of protecting themselves, their homes, and their families. They clearly recognized that law enforcement officers alone could not always be there to defend and protect them, and in the twenty-minutes plus – nationwide average time in which it takes law enforcement to respond to an emergency 911 call,[1] horrible things could happen, even within the presumed sanctity of a person's own home.

Realistically speaking, the same desire to be protected is also omnipresent when a person is in public places, but of course this should come as news to no one. Television and newspapers are filled with accounts of tragic occurrences in which innocent people have lost their lives as a result of violence on the streets and while they were in the presumed safety of public places. Unwilling to be victimized without resisting, many citizens have chosen to take the precaution of arming themselves – both in their homes as well as when they and their families are out in public.

And if you doubt that American citizens are seriously concerned about their safety, consider this: In 2016 alone, 15 million concealed handgun permits were issued to citizens here in the United States – citizens just like you and me. This brings the total estimated number of private citizens holding a valid license to carry a concealed handgun to a staggering 30 million, and this number does not reflect the number of concealed carriers in the five states which do not require permits, registration, or any other form of reporting or documentation. The true number of nationwide concealed carriers is most likely closer to 50 million. More than six percent of the adults in America today have a valid permit to carry a concealed weapon on their person, and in 10 states that number is even higher than ten percent. On any given day in America, approximately one in every twenty-five adults are armed while they are in public. And with so many citizens choosing to arm themselves, what effect has all those guns had on America's crime statistics in the most recent twelve years? Murder rates have fallen from 5.6 to 4.4 per 100,000 people, a 22% drop in murders during the same period of time in which concealed handgun permits increased by 130%. Overall violent crime also decreased by 22% during that same period of time (2003 to 2015). Unfortunately, many of our esteemed anti-gun politicians hesitate to share these types of facts with their constituents, in fact, they ignore them altogether, and for very self-serving reasons. Their anti-gun platforms are absolutely destroyed whenever hard facts are introduced into the equation. ***Note: These statistics are not imaginary. They are taken from a comprehensive report issued by the Government Office Of Accountability and published by the Research Director and the Director Of Communications, as well as statistics gathered by the non-partisan Crime Prevention Research Center.***[8]

For additional impartial, eye-opening facts, visit the web site of The Crime Prevention Research Center at: ***crimeresearch.org.***   In order to maintain their objectivity, the CPRC is not funded, nor do they receive donations from any pro-gun advocate organizations. Their published research is entirely factual, and is not unduly opinionated or influenced by any pro-gun lobby.

Interesting Footnote:

At the time this book is going to press, in my home state of Oklahoma, an interesting bill was just presented on the floor of the State Senate last week. The State Senate had just convened for the opening of the 2017 legislative session, and a pro-gun bill has been introduced right off the bat. Senate Bill #386, sponsored by state Senator Anthony Sykes, would prohibit the use of public tax monies for the funding of lobbying efforts for gun control legislation. Oklahoma residents do not pay taxes so that local elected officials can use the money to push their own private agendas such as their anti-gun political efforts. Second Amendment supporters in Oklahoma are encouraged to contact members of the Senate Public Safety Committee in support of Senate Bill #386. It is anticipated that the bill will pass, and hopefully pave the way for other states to follow suit.

Definition Of Concealed Carry Weapon

For the purpose of any and all references in this book to a concealed weapon, all weapons mentioned or illustrated herein are intended to be; 1) Specifically that of a handgun of any caliber which is capable of firing one or more deadly projectiles (bullets), and is of a size which can be concealed among the carrier's clothing in a clandestine manner, yet readily accessible in time of need. 2) In addition, all references are intended to apply only to those weapons which are purchased legally, carried legally, and in complete accordance with all applicable federal, state, and local laws and ordinances.

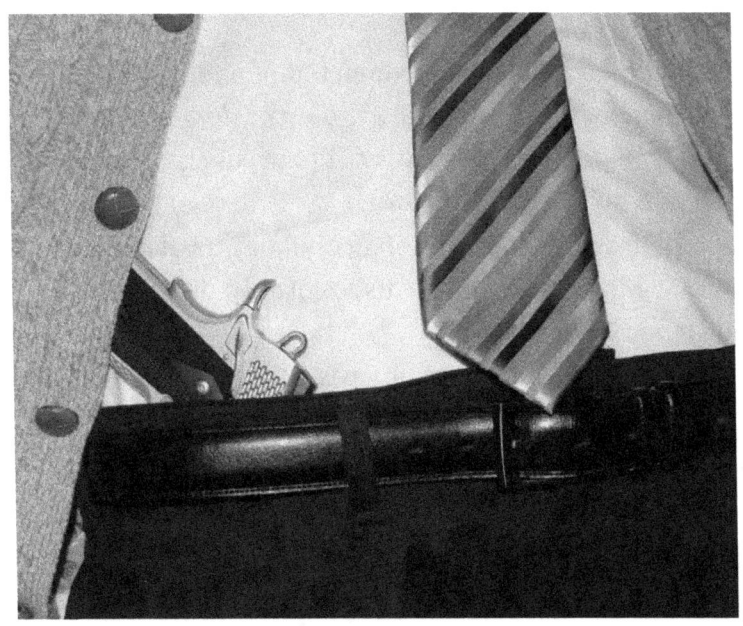

To Carry – Or Not To Carry

In most of the fifty-two United States, a person has the legal right to make the initial purchase of a firearm and to carry a firearm, concealed or otherwise, if they can answer '***Yes***' to all of the following statements:

- I am currently a citizen of the United States.
- I am purchasing the firearm exclusively for my own personal use.
- I am not a fugitive from justice.
- I am twenty-one years of age or older (*this age restriction may vary in some states*).

- I am not under indictment by any court for the commission of a felony.

- I have never been convicted of a felony (*or certain misdemeanors such as spousal abuse or domestic violence*).

- I have no history of being declared mentally defective by a court.

- I am not an abuser of alcohol or illegal drugs.

- I have never been dishonorably discharged from the armed forces.

- I am not subject to any restraining orders.

- I am not now, nor have I ever been a member of any organization which aspires to overthrow the United States Government.

- I have never renounced my United States citizenship, and I am in the United States legally.

Note: When completing form 4473, the applicant has the option of whether or not they are willing to enter their Social Security number on the application. Failure to provide a Social Security number will not affect the processing of the application in any way.

If a potential handgun buyer can answer each of those statements with a '*yes*,' and can pass a background check to verify their legitimacy by their state police or their state bureau of investigation, then they have the legal freedom and constitutional right to purchase a firearm and arm themselves, either while they are in their home, or while they are in public (with certain exceptions and limitations in some states and locales). Most states require a person to have some form of permit in their possession in order to legally carry a weapon on their person, either concealed or otherwise. Other states (five) require no permit or licensing at all, and as long as the possessor of a firearm complies with the law, he or she is legally free to arm themselves.[9] The process for obtaining a permit to legally carry a concealed weapon on your person is very similar in most states that require a permit. A general summary of that procedure is as follows[2]

1) An application must be obtained either from the sheriff's department or downloaded online from the state government's website.

2) The application is filled out, dated, and signed. Most states require an applicant to attend a firearms safety class and obtain a certificate of handgun training prior to the issuance of a permit.

3) The completed application, along with a completion certificate for a handgun training course and the appropriate fees are submitted back to the sheriff's department.

4) Fingerprints of the applicant are made, a photograph is taken, and everything is forwarded by the sheriff's department to the state bureau of investigation or the state police for a thorough evaluation and a background search through the national database for any undeclared criminal history.[10]

5) If everything checks out, the permit is issued. This process can take from fourteen to ninety days, but due to the high number of applications in recent years, most states have streamlined the process and can now issue permits within a thirty day period of time.

As mentioned, this procedure and the specific requirements can vary somewhat by state, and an applicant needs to check the regulations and requirements in the jurisdiction of his/her residence. There are state government web sites which can provide additional information for applicants.

The tremendous surge of new applications in recent years has been spawned in part by disturbing headlines reporting previously unfathomable crimes. After the tragic church shootings which occurred in Texas, Virginia, South Carolina, and Alabama in 2015 and 2016, many churches and synagogues have incorporated an organized security program in which designated deacons, attendants, or other church-appointed personnel are now armed with concealed weapons during most of the scheduled church services. In that way, if a deranged individual decides to start shooting members of the congregation, decisive force, including deadly force, can be taken to hopefully minimize the number of victims in such a tragedy. Some of the larger and more urban churches even employ armed security guards; some of whom are uniformed and some who are dressed in plain clothes so as to blend in with the congregation. In the church that I attend, which is a small, rural country church, an undisclosed number of privately selected persons have been charged with the responsibility of monitoring church security and responding in the case that such an emergency were to occur. The presence of selected armed men among the congregation is secretive in nature, and perfectly invisible to the public eye – as it should be – in order that their presence will not detract in any way from the earnestness of the worship service experience. It's a sad state of affairs when such extreme measures have become necessary in a church. But for a church or similar institution to have no type of emergency plan of response at all would be a betrayal to the trust of the attending congregation, and a terribly negligent disregard of responsibility. Yet it remains a characteristic of human nature to assume that bad things can only happen in '*other places*' and to '*other people.*'

Making the decision as to whether or not a person or persons should take the initial steps to arm themselves when they are in public places is a very personal issue, and undoubtedly unique to the individuals involved. The question of, "**should I or shouldn't I?**" is a question which is so profound that it can only be answered by each individual. '*Gun-packing*' is certainly something that not everyone is psychologically or physiologically capable of doing. A longtime personal friend of mine who lives in a mid-eastern urban area near downtown Philadelphia once told me that he seldom left his home to go shopping or run errands without first arming himself. He said that the reason he armed himself whenever he was in public was simply because it made him feel safer; that regardless of what terrible things might happen, he and his family would not be relegated to becoming the totally helpless victims of random crime. Like me, he has carried a concealed weapon on his person on and off for more than three decades, and thankfully, just like me, he has never yet encountered a situation in which he needed to resort to drawing his weapon. Nevertheless, the feeling of safety and security has been well worth the hundreds of times that we have bothered to discretely arm ourselves before leaving our homes. We need to remember that, just because nothing seriously threatening has personally occurred to either of us in the past is no assurance or guarantee that a deadly encounter will never happen to us, and after all; ***some means of protecting oneself... some plan of defense – even a weak plan – is far superior to having no plan at all.***

No one knows when or where the next tragic event might take place, but we've all heard the horrible accounts of helpless, unarmed victims being systematically executed by merciless madmen one at a time, and some people are just not willing to stand by and let that happen without presenting some form of resistance which carries infinitely more authority and prominence than simply begging and pleading for one's life.

A plan of defense aimed at safeguarding the children of a family's household is a wise precaution as well. There should be a designated "*safe*" room or area within the house for everyone to meet in time of danger, and at a moment's notice. The place should be in a location that is convenient to some sort of an escape; a doorway to the outside, a window in a bedroom, etc. Children should be taught to go there in time of an emergency, whether the emergency is a fire, natural disaster such as a tornado, or a home invasion. Children should also be taught that if they hear a loud argument or a gunshot in some other part of the house, they should never go toward the sound to investigate, despite their concern and curiosity. Instead, they should be taught to flee. There are circumstances in which hiding under a bed is just not safe enough. There are times when the safest thing to do might be to leave the home and flee for a designated neighbor's house. Neighbors should discuss such plans between themselves, share ideas, and know each other's plans. The important thing is to have a plan – whatever plan works the best for you and your family – and to teach that plan to your children. A responsible parent should know their children better than anyone, and they should know how to encourage their children to participate in practice drills and exercises in a serious manner without frightening the children unnecessarily. And while we are on the subject, let's touch base on another very important aspect of armed resistance and defense – and perhaps the ***most*** important aspect of all. ***If evacuation and flight is an option, (especially where children are concerned), getting the family away to safety should always be the primary immediate objective.*** Men can sometimes be irrational and overly confrontational when the sanctity of their home has been invaded. Forcing a confrontation when there are other options is not heroic, it's idiotic. Even inside one's own residence, and even if you are well armed, it's much wiser to flee safely with your family away from impending danger than it is to force an exchange of gunfire, especially when family members or children are within the residence. Bullets can penetrate walls like they were made of paper, and even when family members are hiding in another part of the house they are never completely safe whenever bullets begin to fly. Remember: ***The avoidance of an armed confrontation is always preferable to having any kind of conflict which involves firearms or any other type of weapon for that matter.*** Think about it often, and keep your available options fresh in your mind. In the event of an actual home invasion, there is rarely time to think during the heat of the moment, and certainly no time to formulate a plan. Your reaction to the situation should be pre-programmed in the minds of you and your family, and occur naturally and quickly in the event that such a horrid circumstance should ever come to your house.

Let's touch base on another very important aspect of being armed. However we might consider our own individual justification in arming ourselves, there is **one truth** which remains constant, regardless of the circumstances, and it's a truth which transcends all the feelings of macho-power, authority, and responsibility which descends upon us when we have a gun in our possession. It's a truth which we need to continually remind ourselves: ***Having a permit to carry a concealed weapon on our person does not authorize a private citizen to act as representatives of law enforcement – period!*** Law enforcement personnel are highly trained and experienced professionals who are legally responsible for enforcing the law and protecting the public. They are professionals who have been duly appointed by the people to serve and protect the public. Private citizens are simply that – ***private citizens***. When we choose to arm ourselves while we are in public we are doing so exclusively for the purpose of defending ourselves and protecting our families, and **not** for the purpose of exercising any form of armed authority simply because we are in possession of a firearm! Those individuals who think otherwise are destined for trouble, and perhaps tragedy. It is not our role to become the neighborhood's *Dirty Harry,* or some sort of '*vigilante enforcer*' on a white horse, responding to the rescue and correction of any and all offenses committed within our proximity. Such a mentality is not only dangerous for ourselves, inappropriate intervention, especially while in possession of a firearm, can only lead to the increased

endangerment of those innocent people around us –
negating all the positive reasons of why we have chosen
to arm ourselves in the first place. If you aspire to
become the next '*Bernard Goetz,*'[3] then you are precisely
the reason that some people were not meant to own or
carry a firearm. Remember: **You have the right to use
deadly force for your own protection and for the
protection of your family. You also have the right to
intervene with deadly force to save the life of someone
else.** Beyond that, our rights have very distinct
limitations. History has shown us that our justice system
(*although the best in the world today*) is terribly flawed
when it comes to dispensing justice, and many well-
intentioned individuals have been subjected to
unwarranted litigation and punishment for doing what
they thought was morally and ethically right at the time.
Morally right and legally right are entirely different
animals, and there are underlying reasons why Lady
Justice wears a blindfold. When your armed intervention
is not absolutely necessary to save a life, you'd best keep
your firearm holstered and defuse the situation by
walking away whenever possible.

When a properly trained woman makes the
decision to become the carrier of a concealed weapon she
transforms into a person who is psychologically and
physically no longer a member of the '*weaker*' sex, per se.
While her aggressor might be armed with much greater
physical strength and have ill intentions, a simple firearm
weighing perhaps less than twenty-five ounces can be a

lifesaving miracle which can magically level the playing field when an aggressor seeks to inflict bodily harm. Think of how horrifying it must be for an unarmed woman to face an assailant twice her size in a dark parking lot or alley somewhere with no one nearby to come to her aid and no time to place a call to 911 and wait twenty minutes for help to arrive. If there was a handgun in her purse, it might represent her only means of avoiding the terrible consequence of being raped and murdered – it might represent her only chance to avoid a vicious, and perhaps deadly attack. Thousands of such scenarios have occurred which ended in the tragic death of the assailant's victim. In at least one case, in Dallas, Texas in 2011, a half-empty canister of pepper spray was found near the woman's partially nude body in a downtown building's parking lot. Apparently, the pepper spray did little more than annoy her attacker, and certainly failed miserably in saving her life. If the mother of three had the time and the presence of mind to pull the pepper spray from her purse, she undoubtedly could have had the time to draw and fire a pistol – a maneuver which would have been infinitely more effective in saving her life than the pepper spray. If the woman had been properly trained in the martial arts, perhaps that would have made a difference. But many women lack the physical stature and muscular capability of becoming effectively proficient in the martial arts.[11]

It has to be every woman's worst nightmare — waking up from a deep sleep to find a stranger standing over them.   But such a thing actually happened to an Albuquerque, New Mexico woman who was successful in overpowering and killing a convicted rapist after he broke into her home, climbed into her bed and held a gun to her chest in 2002.

The woman, who has preferred to be identified only as "*Lisa*," is a single mom, Sunday School teacher, and bookkeeper in her early 30's who said she acted only out of instinct, and was driven purely by the desire to survive.   She told police that she was home alone and was asleep in her bedroom about 1:30 a.m. on July 20th, when she woke to find a flashlight pointed toward her face and a masked man straddling her in bed.

"After going to sleep, I was in the dead of sleep. I woke up with a man on top of me," Lisa told investigating police afterward. I immediately just had the reaction to get him off of me at that point. He told me that he had a gun and I could feel it against the left side of my chest. He was restraining me with both of his hands and the gun was lying across my chest and I just took my left hand and I started just pushing him away from me."

Lisa started trying to push him off with her hands and feet, using some martial arts and self-defense techniques which she had learned years before in a self-defense seminar.

"Do you want to die?" he asked.   At that point, something snapped and she sprang into action, Lisa said. In what she described as something like "*a dream state*," she wrestled the .38-caliber revolver away from her 170-

pound attacker and rolled him off the bed and onto the floor. She then grabbed the gun and fired three shots at the man, striking him twice in the upper torso.

The woman and police later learned that the man was 51-year-old Michael Magirl of Albuquerque, a convicted sex offender. Almost 20 years previously he was convicted of 33 burglaries in Clovis, N.M., where he raped a female Air Force Captain while her children slept in an adjacent bedroom. He only served half of a 31-year sentence before being released on parole.

Police say Magirl's car was parked at an apartment project about two blocks from the woman's home, and he had "*rapist tools*" with him, including a flashlight, gloves, and duct tape. Officers seized a backpack, a pillowcase and binoculars from the car. Lisa had just bought a home in Albuquerque, and was in the process of moving on the night the incident happened. There had been a lot of workers in and out of the one-story house earlier that day, as she was in the process of moving in. She went to bed around 11:30 p.m. that night, after checking each door and window to make sure that they were locked. Police say that Magirl appeared to have forced his way into Mira's home through a sliding glass door at a rear patio of the house, where pry marks and a damaged doorjamb were found.

After Lisa fired the gun, she thought she had only injured Magirl. She turned the light on and quickly pulled the pantyhose mask off of his head so that she would be able to identify him, before running to a neighbor's house to call police. Magirl died at the scene, and authorities have classified his death as a justifiable homicide. Police are now investigating Magirl in connection with several other unsolved attacks in the Albuquerque area. Had Lisa not been able to wrestle the gun from her assailant, she would have been raped and possibly murdered – while in the presumed safety and security of her own home of all places.

In the weeks following her assault, Lisa purchased her own handgun for her home, a permit to carry the gun concealed, and has taken shooting lessons at an Albuquerque shooting range near her home.

In the early spring of 1990, my employer at the time, AT&T, had transferred me from the Northern Virginia area to the town of Danville, Virginia on the North Carolina border. Several times I had spoken by telephone to the woman who would become my secretary at my new assignment. Two weeks before I had actually reported to my office in Danville, my secretary worked late one night in order to prepare things for my arrival. Leaving the building well after dark that night, she was abducted in the dark parking lot by two males from Washington, D.C., and taken to a remote wooded area where she was raped repeatedly by both assailants. After they had raped her, they shot her in the head at point blank range with a 9mm handgun and dumped her nude body in the woods a hundred yards from state route 58, which runs easterly from

Danville to the town of South Boston, thinking they had killed her. Miraculously, she survived, and was able to flag down a passing motorist who summoned help. The gunshot had destroyed a massive amount of brain tissue, but surgeons were able to transport her by helicopter to Duke University Hospital in Durham, and save her life. She never recuperated fully, however, and never regained the mental capability of returning to work. When I arrived at my new office, I had lighting installed in the employee parking lot, but it was too little and too late to have helped this unfortunate woman. I heard many testimonies from other employees proclaiming what a wonderful person she had been; kind, generous, and compassionate – attributes which meant nothing to her assailants. I've always wondered if adequate lighting alone would have prevented her abduction, and I've always been of the opinion that a handgun in her purse could have been used to turn the tide of horrible events that happened to her that evening. The two men were captured shortly thereafter, convicted of rape and attempted murder, and both received prison sentences – little consolation to the victim or her family.

In Georgia, in the spring of 2000, George McDonald heard a disturbance coming from his thirteen year-old daughter's bedroom just minutes before 3AM. Before going to investigate, he retrieved a .45-caliber handgun from his bedside drawer. Entering his daughter's bedroom with his handgun and switching on the overhead light, he saw 49 year-old Jeffrey Shields in the process of attempting to rape his daughter. Shields was holding a knife to the young girl's throat when McDonald turned on the overhead light. When Shields stood up to face McDonald, McDonald wasted no time in firing a single shot which killed Shields instantly. Atlanta Police were summoned, and after an investigation ruled that Shields' death had been a justifiable homicide. Shields was on parole at the time of his death after being convicted of raping the twelve year-old child of his next-door neighbor just five years prior. His lengthy rap sheet indicated that he had also been guilty of committing rapes in 1989, 1993, and 1996. The fact that Shields was on parole after having such a long history of sexual battery and abuse, is indicative of the imprudent leniency extended by a justice system – a system which often serves the criminal faction much more conveniently than it serves the judicial interests and well-being of the public.

Each of us have the right to protect ourselves, and we also have the moral right and responsibility to extend our protection to those we love. It is important that a person understand his/her legal rights – especially as those rights pertain to the owners and carriers of firearms. God forbid this type of violence from ever touching our lives – but if it does, are we prepared to deal with it, or are we and our loved ones destined only to become the victims in tomorrow's ten o'clock news?

During a concealed Carry Class in Apache, Oklahoma in 2015, a student who seemed less than enthusiastic about being there, posed the question to the instructor, "What should we be carrying on our person in the way of weapons? Exactly what kind of confrontation should we be prepared to deal with?"

It's a question that was intended to baffle the instructor, and in a way, it did, because there is no simple answer to such a question. The fact is; if we knew precisely what kind of conflict was going to occur, when it was going to occur, and what sort of weapons our assailants would be armed with, perhaps we could then prepare ourselves in the most efficient manner. For example, if our assailant was armed with a knife or a club, we would have the advantage if we were armed with most any caliber of handgun. On the other hand, if our assailants were more than one in number, and they were armed with automatic rifles, perhaps no amount of conventional weaponry would be enough to save the day. It's a question which is impossible to answer because of the innumerable variables involved. Besides, if most of us knew the precise time and place an incident was going to occur, we would certainly avoid going there in the first place.

There are frequent differences of opinion among concealed handgun carriers as well as law enforcement officers as to what handguns and calibers of ammunition are best suited for concealed carry protection. That being said, there are a number of concealed carriers who carry full-sized, semi-automatic pistols as well as several magazines of ammunition on a routine basis. This is another one of those areas in which personal preferences come into play. There are no absolutes, and the individual is going to have to decide what is best for them. Statistics have shown that most confrontations with an assailant which result in shots being fired, usually occur at a distance of between seven and eighteen feet – relatively close range, and the average number of shots fired by a person defending themselves is only three. If this is true, is it really necessary for a concealed carrier to have extra magazines of ammunition on their person? Again, these are the types of questions that are best answered by the intended carrier, and their choice depends greatly on what arrangement provides them with the most confidence and peace of mind in their security and well-being. And to a great degree, that would depend heavily on their level of knowledge of the subject.

The Dangerous False Illusions Of Concealed Carry

When we first consider the possibility of becoming a concealed weapon carrier, images and ideas can often pop into our minds which are completely off-base and can be dangerously misleading. First of all, carrying a concealed weapon, in and of itself, does not assure us that we will automatically be safer wherever we go. Simply possessing a gun makes us no safer than if we had no gun at all, and in some cases having a gun on our person can actually place us further in harm's way. It's the education; the mental preparedness, the training, and the practice which might contribute to our future safe-being. There are misinformed people who think that all they need to do is to purchase a handgun, and get a carry permit, and their level of safety will instantaneously be elevated. The complexities involved with carrying a gun are such that life as a concealed carrier is not that simple, and the folks who think it is are in for a disappointment.

Secondly, the illusion that once an armed bad guy sees that you have a gun pointed at them their backbone will immediately turn to jelly and they will turn tail and flee for their lives... is just another fairy tale. More times than not, if a bad guy has his gun drawn and sees that you have a gun, out of sheer surprise, shock, and terror he will most likely start shooting at you as he runs to get away.

Thirdly, handgun carriers who are under the impression that they can draw their gun on an armed robber and yell, "**Drop your gun!**" ...thinking the bad guy is going to immediately comply with their demand... well... it just doesn't happen that way in real life when a plain-clothed citizen makes such a request. Shouting demands may or may not work for a uniformed police officer, but ninety-nine percent of the time, verbal commands simply don't work at all for John Q. Public... in fact, a shouted verbal command is more than likely going to be the catalyst that initiates the beginning of actual shots being exchanged. There's a simple and brutal truth in those horrifying moments of deadly confrontations; If you are forced to draw your gun against an armed assailant, you should not wait for the person to notice that your gun is drawn – if innocent lives are in eminent danger, including your own, you had better be resolved to using your gun before they use theirs – it's your best chance for surviving traumatic and deadly events such as an armed robbery or a mugging. Your odds of surviving an armed confrontation are reduced exponentially whenever the bad guy is given the opportunity of firing the first shot. The thought process of an armed criminal is already irrational to begin with – their panic causes them to lose their ability to make rational decisions. And when their adrenaline is raging, such as it is during the commission of an armed robbery, their judgment becomes even more impaired and their subsequent actions more unpredictable.   This inability to think rationally combined with the panic of the moment accounts for the reason why so many armed robbers shoot their victims even after the victims have cooperated fully and given them their money. This is an unpleasant fact of life, to be sure, but it is also a fact which has been corroborated many times by eye witness accounts as well as surveillance video footage. Criminals are almost always in a high state of panic while committing a crime, and often become even more panic-stricken when things don't go according to their plans, and you can be sure that they never expected to encounter armed resistance, or they wouldn't have been there in the first place. When they do encounter armed resistance, in their fright and terror, they are likely to think that using their gun is their only hope of getting away. It is important that you know what things might be going through their mind if you find yourself in the middle of a robbery or other armed confrontation. With this in mind, and before you find yourself in such a deadly situation someday…

Look in the mirror and ask yourself this very important question; "Am I really prepared to take the life of an assailant in order to save my own life or perhaps save the life of another innocent person?" If you can answer that question with a resounding, '***yes***,' you just might be a candidate for concealed carry.

The Castle Doctrine

A Castle Doctrine (also known as a castle law or a defense of habitation law) is a legal doctrine that designates a person's home or any legally occupied space where a person might be; such as a vehicle, home, place of business, or office, as a place in which that person has the inherent protection and immunity which permits him or her, in certain circumstances, to use force, up to and including deadly force, to defend and protect himself or herself against an intruder, and to remain free from legal prosecution for the consequences of the force used.

However, it should be noted that this definition of the Castle Law can be somewhat misleading, especially where it says, *"...and to remain free from legal prosecution for the consequences of the force used."* This clause depends entirely on the circumstances involved. A person using deadly force, namely a firearm, is never free from *'legal inquiry,'* such as a court hearing or a grand jury, and whether or not they are exonerated of any or all wrong doings depends entirely on the determination made during these inquiries.

The term, *'castle doctrine'* is most commonly used in the United States, though many other countries have invoked comparable protection principles in their laws.

Before using deadly force, a person may have a duty to retreat in order to avoid violence if one can reasonably do so. Castle doctrines negate the duty to retreat when an individual is assaulted in a place where that individual has a right to be, such as within one's own home. Deadly force may be justified and a defense of justifiable homicide may be applicable, in cases "...when the defender reasonably fears imminent peril of death or serious bodily harm to him or herself or another" [sic]. The castle doctrine is not a defined law that can be invoked, but a set of principles which are incorporated in some form or another in the laws of most jurisdictions within the United States.

Justifiable homicide inside one's home is distinct, as a matter of written law, with a different definition than *'castle doctrine's'* no duty to retreat therefrom. Because the mere occurrence of trespassing—and occasionally an arguably subjective requirement of fear—is sufficient to invoke the castle doctrine, the burden of proof of fact is much less challenging than that of justifying a homicide. With a mere justifiable homicide law, one generally must objectively prove to an inquiry or a court of law, beyond all reasonable doubt, that the intent in the intruder's mind (whether trespassing or not) was to commit violence or a felony. It would be a misconception of law to infer that because a state has a justifiable homicide provision pertaining to one's home, it has the same thing as a castle doctrine, exonerating any duty whatsoever to retreat therefrom. The use of this legal principle in the United States has been controversial in relation to a number of tragic cases in which it has been invoked, including the deaths of Japanese exchange student, Yoshihiro Hattori (October 20, 2012), and Scottish businessman, Andrew de Vries (January 8, 1994). Cases such as these have a horrible way of reminding us that there are severe consequences for the times in which we make hasty and poor decisions. Cases such as these exemplify the fact that gun ownership and poor judgment can sometimes be a lethal and tragic combination. Gun owners would do well to remember that violent occurrences and potential threats can often happen in the blink of an eye, making it necessary for defenders to make critical snap decisions.

Concealed Carry And General Firearm Safety

Responsible firearm owners should know all too well how vitally important the issue of safety is. Most of us have had the subject of firearm safety pounded into our heads since the time we were youngsters and first started handling firearms under dad or grandpop's tutorage. When handled improperly, or handled by untrained people, firearms can be deadly. Even when a person is well-trained overall, when they handle a firearm they are not familiar with, extreme caution should be exercised. Regardless of a person's level of experience or familiarity with handguns, when a person carries a concealed weapon either full time or even part time, over a period of months and years this equates to handling your weapon much more frequently than the average gun owner or enthusiast who might only handle their gun when they visit the shooting range once or twice a year. In all this daily handling, it's easy for a person to become complacent if they don't remind themselves every time they pick up their handgun of the potential danger. This is especially important for a person who handles their firearms so frequently. Over a period of time, actions can become habits, and it's wise to make safety one of those everyday habits that we become accustomed to. Regardless of how familiar our weapons can become to us, a gun is still a gun, with no mind or thought capabilities of its own.   In the right hands, guns can be used to save lives. But we should never lose sight of the fact that guns have the indiscriminate capability of taking the lives of innocent people just as quickly and deadly as they can take the lives of bad guys.   And as redundant as it may seem sometimes, firearm safety should never be taken lightly.

As already emphasized, concealed carriers are gun owners who handle their firearms much more frequently than most gun owners. We handle our handguns each time we wear it when we leave our home, then again when we return home. Many gun owners who are not licensed to carry a concealed weapon may only handle their firearms for a short time during the hunting season, or a trip or two each year to the firing range. During so many months of not handling firearms it is possible for an owner to become unfamiliar with the safety features of their guns, thus setting themselves up for an accident.

Never assume a gun is unloaded - visually check and double check each time you handle a gun

There are a number of firearm safety courses available in most communities in the United States, and up to a few years ago, some of these gun safety courses were taught in high schools here in rural America – before the word, "*gun*" was categorized a dirty word by misinformed and misguided pacifists. The National Rifle Association has promoted responsible firearm safety training since its inception in 1871, and is a valuable resource in directing people to the locations and schedules for classes across the nation.   Many states have adapted the NRA's gun safety lessons and incorporated them as part of their required hunter education safety training. The National Association of Shooting Sports is another good organization with a history of supporting firearm safety training. Contact information for these associations is listed in the "***Resources***" chapter in the back of this book.

There are perpetual rules which govern the handling of firearms that should never be taken lightly. They should be reviewed often, even by seasoned veterans. Before moving on, we'll mention a few of these inviolate rules here. First of all, and most importantly, even when we think that a gun is empty, all firearms should be treated with the same caution and respect that we would extend to a firearm which we know for certain to be loaded, and those sacred, time-honored rules will never become outdated.

(**1**) Loaded or not, always point the weapon in a safe direction, and never point it at anything you don't intend to shoot. Unless you are preparing to shoot, the firearm should be pointed downward toward the floor or the ground, and never under any circumstances should the gun be pointed in the direction of people.

(**2**) Never put your finger on the trigger of any weapon until you are actually preparing to shoot.

(**3**) Never store the weapon in a place accessible to children or potentially accessible to children.

(4) Always consider a weapon to be loaded unless you absolutely know otherwise. Check and double check, and then check once more. If it's a semi-automatic type weapon, remove the gun's magazine – even an empty one – and then check the chamber once more, visually assuring yourself that there is not a cartridge in the chamber.

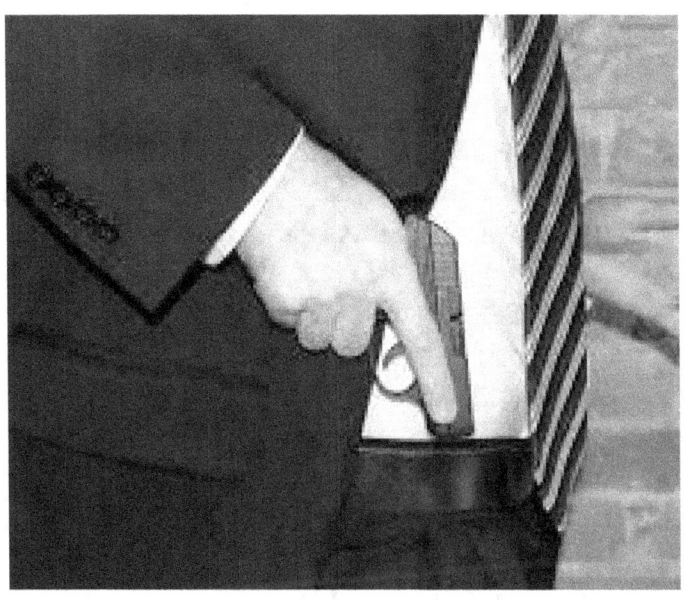

(5) When preparing to shoot, identify your target beyond any shadow of a doubt, and assure yourself that the area behind your target is free of people, pets, and/or property. The possibility of collateral damage must be assessed and assured prior to pulling the trigger – once the shot is fired, it's too late.

From the National Shooting Sports Foundation (NSSF) the traditional 10 golden rules of firearm safety are:

1. **ALWAYS KEEP THE MUZZLE POINTED IN A SAFE DIRECTION**
2. **FIREARMS SHOULD BE UNLOADED WHEN NOT ACTUALLY IN USE**
3. **DON'T RELY ON YOUR GUN'S "*SAFETY*"**
4. **BE SURE OF YOUR TARGET AND WHAT'S BEYOND IT**
5. **USE CORRECT AMMUNITION**
6. **IF YOUR GUN FAILS TO FIRE WHEN THE TRIGGER IS PULLED, HANDLE WITH CARE!**
7. **ALWAYS WEAR EYE AND EAR PROTECTION WHEN SHOOTING**
8. **BE SURE THE BARREL IS CLEAR OF OBSTRUCTIONS BEFORE SHOOTING**
9. **DON'T ALTER OR MODIFY YOUR GUN, AND HAVE GUNS SERVICED REGULARLY**
10. **LEARN THE MECHANICAL AND HANDLING CHARACTERISTICS OF THE FIREARM YOU ARE USING**

These rules apply to anyone handling firearms – and anytime a firearm is admired, passed from one person to another, or in use at the firing range.

One question which seems to be the source of endless debate among concealed weapon carriers who have chosen to carry semi-automatic pistols, is whether or not a person should carry their weapon in their holster or pocket in a cocked and locked condition, that is, with a live round in the chamber. Proponents for *'live-round carry'* would argue that if they needed to use their weapon at a moment's notice, precious time would be lost if it was necessary to rack a live round into the chamber prior to deployment – that the weapon is useless when carried in such a manner. These people usually carry their weapons in the same manner as most policemen; *'cocked and locked,'* and depend exclusively on a safety feature of the gun in order to avoid an accidental discharge (such as a thumb safety).[12]

On the other hand, some people carry their weapons un-cocked, with a live round in the chamber, and simply cock the hammer in the same motion as they are drawing and raising their weapon to a shooting position. But many of the newer semi-automatic pistols are *"striker-fired,"* meaning that there is no external hammer to be cocked. Some striker-fired pistols (such as the Smith & Wesson M&P Shield) have no thumb safety. These are *"double action"* type pistols, some of which rely primarily on a thumb-engaged safety if the pistol is so equipped. As mentioned, some of these pistols are equipped with no safety feature at all, and the only true safety is having no live round in the chamber. (*An exception would be those weapons equipped with a 'de-cocker,'*) It seems that whenever the topic comes up for discussion there are people in both schools who feel very strongly that their method of carrying their gun is superior to all other options – at least for them. From my point of view, I feel strongly that each carrier should be intimately familiar with the weapon they carry, as well as all of the safety features associated with that particular handgun, and in accordance with that familiarity, they should feel absolute confidence in whatever mode they choose to carry their gun. Of the two handguns which I carry most often, one is a *double action* type semi-automatic, which also has an external hammer. When I carry this gun as my concealed weapon, I carry a live round in the chamber with the hammer relaxed to the '*un-cocked*' position, (*I have a de-cocker on my primary carry handgun*) and in this manner, I am completely assured that there is no chance of an accidental discharge, yet the gun can readily be fired by squeezing the trigger. The second handgun which I carry is a revolver. I carry it un-cocked in the holster, and if needed, I must fire it in a double-action mode, or manually cock the hammer. Whatever means and condition a person might choose to carry their handgun, there are no acceptable excuses for accidents. ***If a handgun cannot be carried or handled safely, it should not be carried or handled at all.***

In addition to the many safety considerations of carrying concealed weapons, there are also some important '*unwritten*' rules for behavior which must be considered and adhered to by all responsible handgun carriers. These are rules which should be unnecessary to even mention here, but on the off chance that someone is unaware of these rules of behavior, I'll touch base on a few of the most important ones, to hopefully refresh these priorities in our minds.

I'm specifically referring to a concealed weapon carrier's conduct here. A successful and responsible carrier of a concealed weapon will carry his or her handgun without the people around them having a clue that they are armed. After all, that's the goal of discrete **concealed** carry, isn't it? Unnecessarily brandishing a firearm in public is childish behavior, and unacceptable for a concealed carrier, and in most states there are laws which specifically prohibit the brandishing of firearms. '**Brandishing**,' according to the dictionary, means: *"to wave or flourish something, especially a weapon, as a threat or in anger or excitement."* Brandishing has been interpreted by courts to also include the holding of a weapon in a person's hand unnecessarily.[13]

It's wise to tell as few people as possible that you are carrying a weapon on your person – and that goes equally as well for the spouse of a concealed carrier. Boasting about having a firearm in your possession, or boasting that your spouse is carrying a weapon can lead to all sorts of unnecessary problems. Undoubtedly, there are criminals who would welcome knowing who owned guns in a given crowd of people and who didn't. That's equally as true for firearms that are kept in the household as it is for weapons carried by concealed carriers. Burglars would be happy to target a home in which they could hope to steal a firearm or two. About 1.4 million firearms were stolen during household burglaries and other property crimes over the six-year period from 2005 through 2010, according to a report released by the Justice Department's Bureau of Justice Statistics (BJS). This number represents an estimated average of 232,400 firearms stolen each year — approximately 172,000 were stolen during burglaries and 60,300 were stolen during the commission of other property crimes. As you might expect, handguns were the most commonly stolen type of firearm from 2005 through 2010. At least one handgun was stolen in 63 percent of the household burglaries and 68 percent of all other property crimes involving firearm theft. More than one gun was stolen from each home in 39 percent of the burglaries, and 15 percent of all the other property crimes which involved gun theft. Suffice to say, handguns have proved to be attractive objects of theft among burglars and other lawbreakers.

Open Carry

"*Open Carry*" is another issue altogether. Even in the states and localities where such a thing is legal, and the carrier is perfectly within his or her lawful rights to do so, the precise allure and psychological attraction behind such a thing eludes me to some extent, probably because of so many years of being inconspicuous in the manner in which I carried my own handguns. But there are times in which I can understand the reasons for open carry, such as camping, hiking, and hunting while in bear or hog country. I have a close friend who is a volunteer auxiliary policeman and a member of the County's Emergency Response Team, and he carries his handgun openly on a routine basis, which I can easily understand.

A month ago, my wife and I saw a man in our local Walmart who was carrying a holstered, full-sized Colt 1911 (One of the larger semi-automatic handguns), with four magazine pouches on his belt. It's perfectly legal for him to carry openly here in Oklahoma despite the fact that I fail to understand exactly why a person would want to do such a thing, and draw unnecessary attention to themselves in the process.

Open carry, although a legal right in most states, may not be everyone's cup of tea

In public places, the open presence of a gun can often make some people nervous, if not downright frightened, and I have no desire to frighten people unnecessarily or unwittingly boast of the fact that I'm carrying a firearm. My decision to carry a weapon is my own personal business, and I'm much more comfortable in knowing that my status of being armed is not openly broadcast to the world around me. However, there are a representative number of legally responsible citizens who feel otherwise, and as long as their open carry is in accordance with the law, so be it. The states in which open carry is legal are illustrated in the following chart[4]:

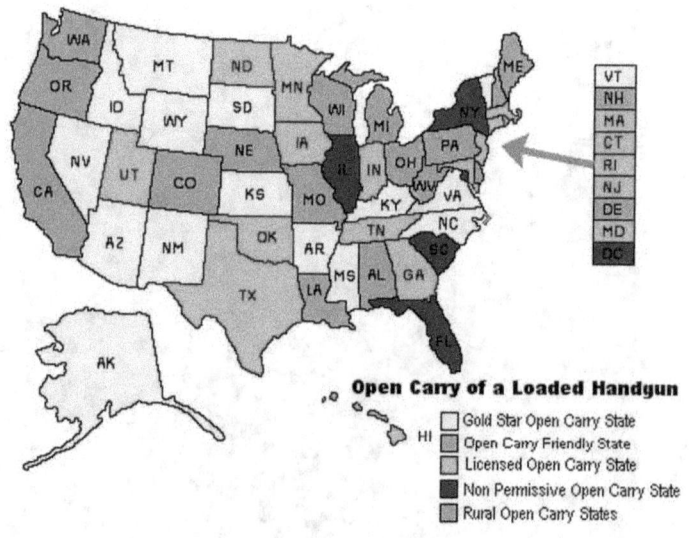

Open Carry of a Loaded Handgun

☐ Gold Star Open Carry State
☐ Open Carry Friendly State
☐ Licensed Open Carry State
■ Non Permissive Open Carry State
■ Rural Open Carry States

In June of 2015, Texas Governor Greg Abbott signed a bill into law permitting the open carry of handguns by those persons who are in possession of a handgun permit. In Texas, in order to openly carry a gun, you have to have a concealed-handgun license on your person. In addition, you have to be at least 21 years of age, and you have to have a clean criminal history as well as an untainted psychological record. You also have to complete a day of classroom training and pass a shooting competency test in the presence of a certified instructor – same is true in Oklahoma as well as many other states.

It should be noted that even in the states where open carry is legal, certain restrictions apply, and it still remains the right of the property owner to deny access to someone who is carrying a gun if they choose to do so. It is the individual carrier's responsibility to keep abreast of applicable laws and ordinances which may prohibit open carry in certain jurisdictions.

In case you haven't figured it out already, the definition of *"open carry"* by the lawmakers of most states is pretty simple and straight forward. If the weapon is **completely** hidden, it's considered to be concealed carry. If **any part** of the weapon is visible, it's considered open carry. Simple enough, huh? Well, it's not that simple everywhere. As could probably be expected, brilliant California lawmakers have found a way to confound the open carry practice to an extreme in most jurisdictions there. For example, in California in order to open carry in most locations, the weapon must be **fully exposed**, with no part of the gun or its components hidden from sight. Taken literally, this makes it illegal to openly carry a handgun in a holster, because a portion of the handgun would be hidden by the holster itself.　In addition, the weapon must be completely **unloaded** at all times, and if it uses a magazine, said magazine must also be fully exposed (*as it's considered to be part of the firearm*).　To add further confusion as to the actual intentions of lawmakers in California, revolver speed-loaders don't fall under this restriction.　How could a handgun be carried "**fully exposed**," unless it was suspended by a string around the carrier's neck?　And... of what use is an unloaded gun anyway?

Virginia provides us with another example of ambiguous guidelines.　Lawmakers there say that in order to be called "*open carry*," the weapon has to be "**easily identified**" as a firearm, so that leaves the actual identification of a handgun open to the interpretation of the individual observer, depending on how much of the weapon is visible to them at the time as well as how familiar they are with what a handgun looks like.　I mention these two examples specifically to illustrate the fact that the concealed carry laws and the open carry laws can vary drastically from one state to another.　A separate book could be written to detail the specific handgun laws and regulations of each state and each jurisdiction.　But because these laws and regulations change so frequently, the book would be outdated before the ink dried.　In order to avoid unnecessary headaches and possible mitigating legal ramifications, you should always **familiarize yourself with the laws in the**

**specific jurisdiction in which you will be carrying –
before you carry – either open, or concealed.**

Note: All of these confusing regulations emphasize the
importance of discrete concealed carry. If no one is
aware of the fact that you are carrying, it's extremely
unlikely that you will draw attention to yourself and be
cited for any unintentional violations.

I have used California and Virginia as examples of
how complicated and unclear laws pertaining to carried
handguns can be, but there are other states that also
provide us with extremely fuzzy regulations. Texas is
often thought to be a wild and wooly *'cowboy'* state. In
actuality, Texas has very stringent regulations when it
comes to concealed carry.

The Perfect Killing Fields

Have you ever noticed that the preferred locations where gun-wielding, cowardly maniacs seek to carry out their evilment on an innocent public just happens to be the very locations in which it is least likely that the perpetrators will encounter any form of armed resistance? With increasing frequency, we have seen these horrible tragedies occurring at schools and colleges, armed forces recruiting offices, churches, shopping malls, airports, offices, and other places which have traditionally been thought of as being among the safest places in our world today. It's no accident that these deviants would choose such places to carry out their evilment. In fact, such places are obviously chosen after careful planning.

Throughout the biggest portion of the twentieth century, the general populous has always felt relatively safe when they were in public places here in our modern-day western world. In the past, there was no justifiable reason for anyone to be on their guard or ill at ease when they went shopping, ran errands, or visited their sacred institutions of worship. But as history has shown us, things are always subject to change – and change they did. In 1986, a man by the name of Patrick Sherrill[5] would commit a crime which would send shockwaves of horror across the nation and have far-reaching implications, forever changing our conceptions and impressions of what was considered safe and what was not.

On August 20th of that year, Sherrill entered the post office in the quiet town of Edmond, Oklahoma, (the perceived epicenter of America's Bible belt) shooting twenty postal employees as they worked, fourteen of them fatally. Then, he turned his gun on himself and committed suicide. In his sickened actions, Sherrill had initiated a catalyst of evil, and established a precedent in which other deranged gunmen would come along to follow in his footsteps. Five additional shootings would occur in post offices in the United States between 1991 and 2006 which took the innocent lives of another twenty victims, coining the repugnant and discreditable term, *'going postal'* somewhere along the way.

The demented minds of the people who conceive and carry out such nightmarish plots are thought to be completely insane, yet the perpetrators are obviously mindful enough of their own safety that they plot to carry out these atrocities in locations where they are least likely to encounter citizens who are armed. Even in their evil-minded desperation, they seem to possess an innate, gut-level concern for their own personal safety. Meanwhile, honest, law-abiding citizens go about their daily business, coming into these very places as lambs to the slaughter, perfectly unaware of what might happen to them or their families. The general public is seldom prepared for such atrocities because we deem them unimaginable until they actually happen.

Knowing that such horrible things have occurred in these supposed *'gun free'* zones, as law-abiding citizens and carriers of concealed weapons, how are we to react to signs on doorways which announce that firearms are prohibited inside? Of course we have the option of leaving our firearms in our automobiles, or not even carrying them with us on any particular day. Because our firearms are concealed on our person, we also have the option of ignoring such idiotic signs and going about our business as normal. In the worst case scenario, if our weapons are accidently seen by someone of authority, they will most likely say nothing at all. On rare occasions an armed patron might be asked to leave the premises. As mentioned in an earlier chapter, if we are asked to leave, we should politely do so without hesitation and without being rude or making any kind of public scene. There are many people in society today who simply do not understand what's happening in America and why some of us have chosen to arm ourselves. Quite possibly, they have been poisoned by the liberal anti-gun rhetoric, and simply do not understand that everyone with a gun is not one of the bad guys. Bringing a concealed firearm into a place where weapons are banned is another of the many choices that the concealed carrier will be facing in the pursuit of his or her everyday business.

I had a dentist appointment a couple of weeks ago in a nearby town. While still seated in my car, and before going inside the building, I noticed a sign on the front door which banned bringing guns inside (something which I usually disregard completely). For reasons I can't explain or recall, on that particular day I removed my handgun from my holster and placed it in the center console of my automobile before going inside. Sitting in the dentist's chair, I noticed that he was smiling and staring at my empty holster. To ease any concerns he might have had, I told him that my handgun was out in my car. He explained why his company *(My Dentist, Inc.)* had mandated that all of their chain locations ban the presence of firearms on their premises, and it was an explanation which left me shaking my head in disgust. According to him, in one of their nationwide offices, a patron was showing his handgun to one of the dentists and in the process of passing the gun to the dentist, it accidently discharged, blowing a hole in the wall and frightening everyone who was within hearing distance at the time. I won't even begin to comment on the idiocy of everything the gun-toting patron did wrong in this case. Suffice to say, sometimes an ignorant concealed weapon carrier can do things which can unwittingly taint the image of all carriers. The responsibility that each concealed carrier has when he or she is armed should never be taken casually. Like it or not, when we are armed, we represent the entire concealed carry community, at least in the eyes of the general public.

Incidents such as that are a discredit to all concealed handgun carriers, and can only lead to additional businesses putting up signs which prohibit the presence of firearms on their premises. There are plenty of occasions when we know ahead of time that we will be entering establishments such as courthouses and schools, and on those types of days we can avoid negative situations completely by simply exercising good judgment and leaving our weapons at home or in the car.

"Shucks, we can't go in here!"   "Good! We'll be safe here!"

Always remember that when a concealed weapons carrier goes afoul of the rules of proper behavior and does something that is childishly stupid enough to be newsworthy, you can bet that the anti-gun extremists and the leftist news media will use the incident as fuel for their anti-gun propaganda whenever and wherever they can. Gun owners and concealed weapons carriers are under the spotlight, and it comes as a blemish to all of us whenever someone conducts themselves in such a disgraceful, ignorant manner. Unfortunately, the largest percentage of people in the general public are naïve enough to believe just about anything they read in print or see on the ten o'clock news.

The Washington Navy Yard, situated on the banks of the Anacostia River near the confluence of the Potomac River in Washington, D.C., conjures up impressions of being a veritable bastion of safety – a personification of security – a place which could easily be considered as being '*untouchable*' by the evilment of crime simply by what the place has always symbolized in our minds – a place representative of the sovereign security and protective vigilance of our nation's armed forces. After all, the Navy Yard is located adjacent to the Washington Marine Barracks and within sight of the Capitol dome; the visual symbol and hallmark of free America. Yet, at 8:20 AM on the morning of September 16th, 2013, one Aaron Alexis, a 34-year-old civilian contractor, entered Building Number 197 at the Washington Navy Yard and began shooting at victims randomly with an AR-15 rifle and a Glock semi-automatic 9mm handgun and indiscriminately killed a dozen people before police arrived and killed him.

The Navy Yard shooting is another example of our misconceptions regarding when and where we could consider ourselves to be completely safe, and immune from any type of deadly violence. The innocent people who were killed there that day caused us, as a nation, to further examine our interpretations of precisely what locations we could reasonably consider as being safe.   It is disturbingly disconcerting to think that there are no longer any places that are one hundred percent immune from the potential of this type of pure evilness. If any of Alexis' victims had been armed, perhaps the number of fatalities would have been lessened – who knows? The hard fact is, the shooting sprees of madmen have the potential of impacting our lives at any time, and in any place, and these types of atrocities have happened with such unforeseen frequency, that the victims are sometimes people we know personally…

My wife's cousin had his own thriving lawn maintenance business near Gaithersburg, Maryland. James L. Buchanan[6] was loved by all who knew him. He was an honest, hard-working man who had always worked long hours at his newly established business, and on the day in point he was mowing the lawn of a car dealership. On that fateful day, October 3, 2002, John Allen Muhammad and Lee Boyd Malvo, known also as the D.C. Snipers, shot and killed him as he was pushing a push-type lawnmower along the curbside in Rockville, Maryland. He was chosen as a victim arbitrarily by these fiends as he was dutifully and innocently involved in his profession.   There was no reason that John Allen Muhammad and Lee Boyd Malvo chose Mr. Buchanan as a victim, other than the fact that when they saw him on that particular day, he was an easy target and completely unaware that he was in the crosshairs of Muhammad's scoped Bushmaster rifle.

It is impossible for me to describe the pain and devastation experienced by Buchanan's family in the aftermath of his tragic murder. My wife received the terrible phone call the following morning, and we both sat there in disbelief.

John Allen Muhammad was twice divorced; his second ex-wife, Mildred Muhammad, sought and was granted a restraining order. Muhammad had been arrested on federal charges of violating the restraining order by possessing a weapon (which he purchased illegally). Under federal law, those with restraining orders are prohibited from purchasing or possessing firearms of any type, as per the Lautenberg Amendment to the Gun Control Act of 1968.[14] He was later convicted of multiple murders and executed for his crimes.

Carrying a concealed weapon does not automatically make us safer when we are in public, nor does it assure us that we will be immune from being the arbitrary victim of someone's insanity. It does, however provide us with a small measure of peace of mind in knowing that if we are targeted by an armed madman, and if we do have an opportunity to make a stand and fight back – we can. Fighting back and making a stand against crime is not always an option that we have, even when we are armed.

In 2010, my daughter's 79-year old father-in-law, Clyde (Jack) Dellinger, owned and operated a lawnmower and small engine repair shop on the same rural Virginia property where he lived, and merely yards from where my daughter and her family lived. His business transactions in this rural Virginia neighborhood were almost exclusively carried out in cash, and he was known to carry a large amount of cash on his person. Jack was a good-hearted man, well-loved by his family, his neighbors, and the members of his church. He always worked very hard – an undeniable asset to his community in Castleton, Virginia. But in the drug-influenced mind of a career criminal who lived in the same county, Jack Dellinger was nothing but a target – someone who possessed enough money to possibly finance his drug addiction for a few weeks.

Thomas L. Hicks was a career criminal with no respect for the property or the lives of other persons – he only cared about getting his hands on the money necessary to buy his drugs. He plotted to rob Dellinger. Jack Dellinger felt sorry for the 62-year old Hicks, and even hired him on to do odd jobs around the repair shop – yet all the time Hicks was planning his crime, and on June 10th, he shot Dellinger at point blank range, right between the eyes with a .380 handgun and robbed him. The gunshot had broken the frame of Dellinger's glasses, penetrated the skull, and destroyed a massive amount of brain tissue – Dellinger pretended to be dead, yet miraculously he lived. My daughter and my son-in-law discovered him lying on the ground near his shop when they returned home with their children from grocery shopping. They immediately placed a call to 911, summoning paramedics and police. Jack remained conscious long enough to give police a full account of who had shot and robbed him. Jack was airlifted to a hospital where surgeons were successful in saving his life, and Hicks was located and arrested two days later. He was charged with robbery and attempted murder and held in a Culpeper County jail without bail, to await trial.

Thomas Lee Hicks

At a hearing on August 3rd, when asked if Hicks was the person who shot and robbed him, Dellinger was quoted by Sheriff Connie C. Smith as saying, "That is him," as Dellinger pointed to Hicks in the courtroom. "He looks different, now that he's cleaned up, but that is him." Dellinger's daughter-in-law, Paula Dellinger, (my daughter) who was also at the preliminary hearing, also gave testimony. Other damaging testimony in the two-day trial included that of Hicks' wife, Barbara, who told the court that Hicks had said to her earlier on the day of the shooting that "I'm going to collect money or kill the guy."

Jack Dellinger was never the same after the shooting, and he died the following January. Jack was unarmed when he was attacked by Hicks, and even if he had been armed it is doubtful that he would have been able to protect himself because of the extent to which he had come to trust Hicks. Even though Hicks was ultimately found guilty of his crimes, he had literally destroyed the Dellinger family, and life would never be the same for them again.

For women, the purse remains the most popular means of effectively carrying and concealing their personal weapon

Concealment – In A World Of Fashion

Generally speaking, the smaller the weapon, the more options that are available for concealment – it only makes sense. Ladies who regularly carry a purse or wear a fanny pack or a loose-fitting sweatshirt are well-outfitted for concealed carry from the very onset, and one step ahead of the game. In the case of men, things can be somewhat more complicated at times. A man has many concealed carry options at his disposal during the winter months because of the additional layers of clothing worn during that time of year. Summer months, however, can often present a very real concealment challenge. During the warmer months, men wear fewer clothes, and therefore have few other options available to them other than the belt holster, with a loose-fitting shirt worn to cover his weapon, or possibly an ankle holster (*if he's one of the men who can tolerate wearing such a thing*). That said, there are a large variety of good holsters on the market to suit almost all concealment needs. They are made from a variety of materials including leather, cordura, nylon, and polymer or kydex. Holsters that are worn outside the waist band (OWB), inside the waist band (IWB), and holsters that are worn at the center of the back (COB) are available in a number of different orientations and materials. If a person is going to carry a concealed weapon regularly, comfort and accessibility are of the utmost importance, and once you've been a concealed carrier for a short time, you'll know exactly which clothes in your closet are best suited for concealing your firearm. I used to think that '*vanity*' in the way a person dressed was a characteristic exclusive to women. In recent years I've changed my opinion somewhat, and come to recognize that men can sometimes practice vanity to a much greater extent than I ever realized. That said, I'll confess to spending a little more time in front of a mirror myself when I'm preparing to go out in public as a concealed weapon carrier. I suppose I can rationalize that the excess time is justifiable whenever a man is making certain that his handgun is properly concealed.

"Belly bands" or "Waistband holsters" are gaining popularity among concealed carriers

Elastic waistband holsters are also a viable option for concealed carry, and they are growing in popularity, not only because of their comfort, but also their effectiveness. With a loose-fitting shirt or blouse worn over this arrangement, concealment is quite effective – for men as well as women. Shoulder holster systems are also a time-honored and viable alternative, especially for a man. When a loose-fitting shirt, jacket, or a blazer is worn, it is practically impossible to see any indication of a holster system or weapon being carried inside. There is an added bonus with a shoulder holster system that is worthy of mention – they are arguably the most comfortable means of carrying the larger and heavier firearms such as the Colt 1911, Sig Sauer P226, CZ-75, or most full-sized .45 caliber handguns as well as large-framed revolvers. Shoulder holster systems have been around for more than a century, and they can vary greatly in price, quality, and functionality. Ranging in cost from $24.95 for some cordura and nylon models to more than $300 for some of the fancier leather versions, there are a wide range of products available, including the more expensive custom-made and custom fitted models. My experience in using the nylon and cordura systems has given me the opinion that they have been a waste of money in my own personal circumstances. For me, they are suitable only for carrying the smaller and lighter handguns.

A person who was not so prudent with their money could opt for holster systems made from exotic skins such as ostrich, alligator, shark, and elephant, and easily push the price tag of a shoulder holster system up into the $400 - $600 range, although I can't understand why a person would spend so much money for a *'fancily tooled'* and engraved holster that is intended to be concealed. I do not mean to beat a dead horse here, but I must stress that personal comfort is vitally important – just as important as concealment itself. If you don't believe me, try sitting in a two-hour business meeting with a handgun poking you in some uncomfortable place. It can be miserable.

There is a wide range of less expensive systems available at some of the internet marketplaces such as eBay© and Amazon,© but buying one without actually trying it on can be risky business. If a person is patient, and searches the auction sites, they can occasionally run upon a bargain. I purchased one of my shoulder holster systems from an estate sale, for less than forty dollars. When it was new, it retailed for almost $180. The leather or kydex holsters for most handguns are molded for that particular handgun, and are not available in a *'one size fits all.'*

Custom tooled leather belt holster

The shoulder holster system is perhaps the most comfortable of all carry methods of carrying larger handguns, but requires an over-shirt, jacket, or blazer in order to conceal a handgun

Heavier pistols such as the Beretta 92FS, Colt 1911, or the CZ 75B can feel as though you are carrying an anvil on your hip when they are carried for long periods in a traditional belt-slide holster, and because of their size it is impractical to carry them inside the waistband. Heavy handguns worn on the hip have also been known to cause a man's pants to sag. This is another of the many reasons that smaller and lighter handguns are so popular among concealed carriers.

Four of my personal handguns are among my favorites for concealed carry purposes; a .45ACP, a .357 magnum revolver, a 9mm, and the smallest, a .380ACP. During most situations when I am in public, I tend to have the highest level of confidence in the more powerful caliber .45ACP, but this handgun is considerably larger and heavier than the revolver, the 9mm, or the .380. Nevertheless, my goal each time I go out in public is to carry the largest caliber handgun that I can comfortably carry concealed, which depends greatly on the particular clothing I will be wearing on that day. If I will be wearing a thick belt along with a jacket or an over-shirt, the heavier mass weight of the .45ACP presents no problem to my personal comfort or my ability to keep the handgun completely concealed. But when I will be wearing lighter clothing or more formal attire with a thin cloth belt, the smaller .380 is my best option by far. Here again, there are some occasions in which a shoulder holster system works perfectly for comfort as well as concealment. It's a matter of doing the proper planning before you leave your home, and making the selections which best suit your comfort and your needs.

For men, there are special-purpose concealment vests available which have a holster pocket or pouch sewn permanently in the inside of the vest. There are also jackets available with this same feature, but most outerwear that is designed and made exclusively for concealed carry purposes can often carry a hefty price tag. For example, one retail outlet which specializes in concealed carry apparel offers a vest for $240 which would normally retail for about $75 at one of the non-specialty outlets. There are probably an ample amount of appropriate garments in every man's current wardrobe to conceal his handgun effectively without having to fork out additional money for "*specialty apparel.*"

Note:

If you are a newcomer to concealed carry, once you have purchased your handgun and decided exactly which way is the best way for you to carry it on your person, it is wise to practice carrying it in your home to make sure the method you've selected is the most comfortable and the most natural-feeling for you. This could save you a lot of aggravation and discomfort down the road, as well as saving you money. Once we are in public, there are often times when we do not have the freedom to make adjustments to our holsters without being obvious. When you have found your most comfortable means of carrying, after a short amount of time, you will become so accustomed to the presence of your handgun on your body that you'll feel perfectly naked without it – providing you have chosen a comfortable carry system to begin with.   My smallest 9mm concealed carry pistol weighs less than fourteen ounces when loaded with a full seven-cartridge magazine, so most of the time I hardly recognize the fact that I'm armed. Other times, I carry a .45 caliber handgun which weighs thirty-five ounces, and requires a shoulder holster system in order to be carried comfortably.

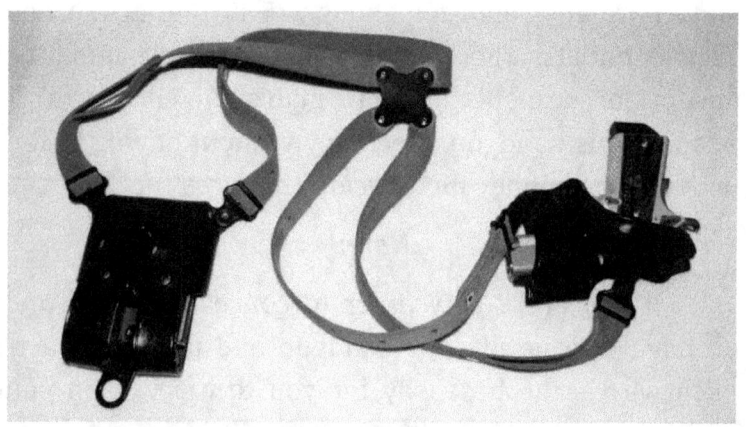

Even the heavier handguns and full magazines can be carried comfortably in a shoulder holster system

When all is said and done, personal comfort may be the determining factor as to whether or not you will carry your handgun with you in a particular circumstance or on any given day. As I mentioned earlier, generally speaking, most men are not very vain... Okay, I'll take that back... **'*Some*'** men are not very vain – that is, until it comes to how they dress when they will be carrying a concealed firearm on their person. When it comes to concealed carry, it's not about vanity, it's about effectiveness. Once you're ready to leave your residence and go out in public, it doesn't hurt to spend an extra moment or two looking at yourself in the mirror to make sure your concealed weapon is in fact, concealed. And on those occasions when you would like a second opinion, it's no blemish on your ego to ask for your spouse's opinion.

In warmer weather the tee shirt holster can be a desirable option as well as a comfortable means of carrying

Concealed carry is a lifestyle in which it can take some initial practice before you become both comfortable and effective in the art of concealment.

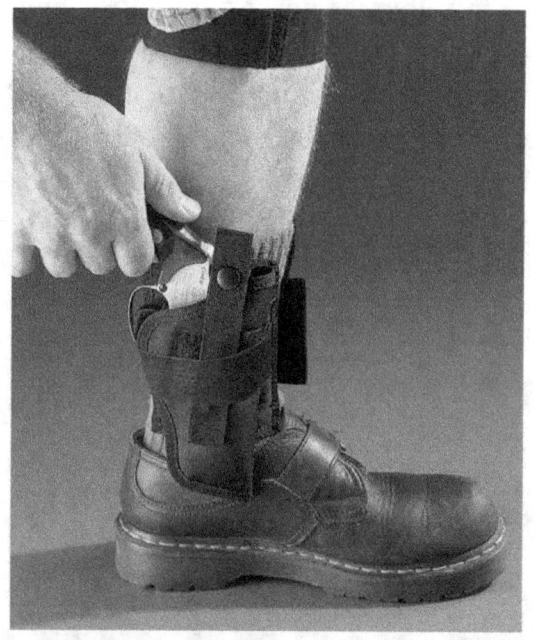

Ankle holsters can be effective, but they can also be quite uncomfortable for some men

Ankle holsters work well for some concealed carriers, although the one time that I tried one, they did not work well on my skinny ankles, and in my case I found them to be extremely uncomfortable and awkward when walking.   Other folks just don't seem to mind the discomfort, and they are a popular option when used with today's lightweight pistols and revolvers.

It's also important to note that ankle holsters are impractical for men who enjoy wearing blue jeans. The two simply don't go together for reasons which are obvious. For the same reasons, holsters which are designed to be worn inside the pants, in a man's groin area or on his hip, are also uncomfortable and impractical in my own opinion.

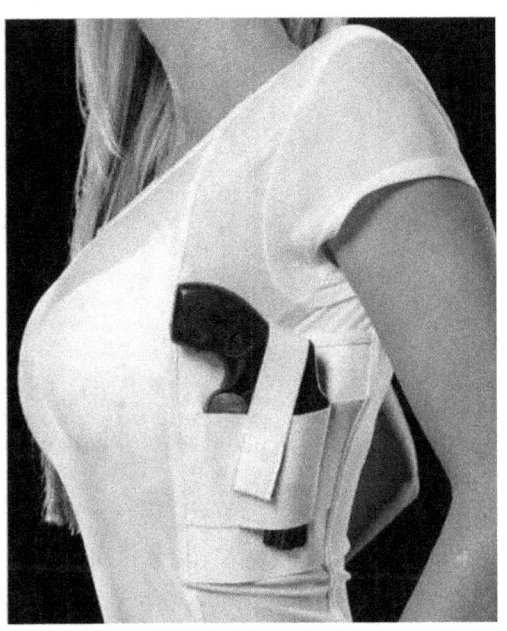

An undergarment holster can work well for women who choose not to carry a purse with them

Tight-fitting clothing can sometimes be a dead giveaway that a firearm is concealed underneath. With concealment being such a major concern, concealed carriers should make every effort to keep their weapon from being "***fingerprinted***" by their garments for the public to see under their clothing, as in the picture on the following page. For the concealed carrier, loose-fitting clothing is always more effective in concealment. It has already been stated previously that the smaller the handgun is, the easier it is to conceal. Unconsciously, I have taken up the habit of studying people in public when I'm running errands or shopping, and it never fails to astonish me when I see some of the ineffective ways in which some people carry their "**concealed**" weapons.

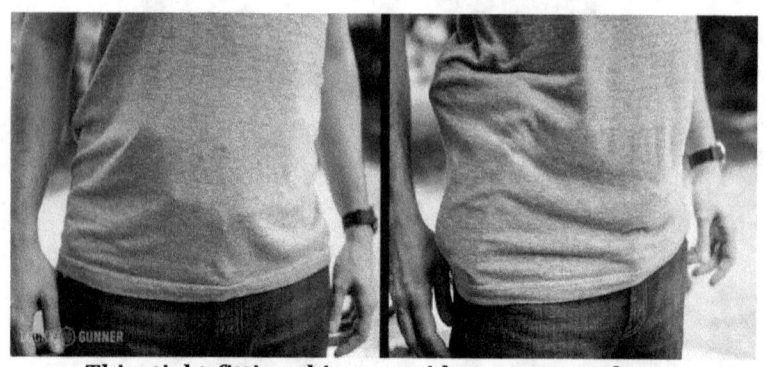

Thin, tight-fitting shirts provide poor concealment

With this in mind, concealed carriers would do well to avoid tight-fitting clothing – especially shirts. This is one of the challenges facing concealed carriers during the warmer months of the year, when the temperature mandates that we wear lighter clothing and fewer layers. Nevertheless, even in hot weather, a loose-fitting shirt can address the situation perfectly. As for women, the same general principles apply: *Loose-fitting clothing is always best when considering concealment,* regardless of whether the lady is wearing a bra holster, waistband holster, or a conventional belt-slide holster on her hip. I cannot imagine how a woman could possibly find a panty holster comfortable – perhaps I'm missing something, but as I stated earlier, I would think the most comfortable option for a woman would be to carry her handgun in her purse or fanny pack. Most of the women I know who are concealed carriers choose to carry their handguns in their purse, for reasons which, in my opinion, are entirely understandable.

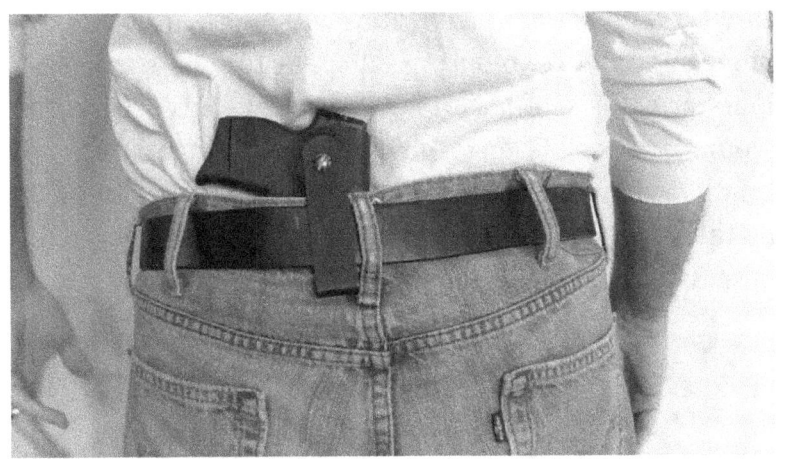

Holsters worn at the small of the back (SOB) work well for some people, and are easily removed when preparing to drive a vehicle or ride for long distances

An entire industry has been established to focus on the production and sale of the countless options which enable us to carry our weapons in a comfortably concealed manner. There are ankle holsters, waistband holsters, shoulder holsters, purse holsters, bra holsters, panty holsters, pocket, wrist, thigh, belt, and boot holsters, and the list goes on. For people who have limited funds, so many different options can add to the confusion of making selections that are practical as well as affordable. There are several things to consider which might help to minimize the expense involved, such as purchasing a used holster.

Visit your local firing range as often as time will permit. Seek the counsel and advice of experienced shooters as well as the advice of veteran concealed carriers. If there are pistol clubs within proximity of your home it would be money well-spent to join, if not on a long term basis, at least temporarily. In this scenario, it would be possible for a novice to shoot many different brands and models of firearms and have a first-hand look at the concealment options that have been chosen by others before making a decision.

A large selection of holster types are available for the concealed carrier

Most firearm enthusiasts are more than willing to share their expertise with newcomers as well as allowing interested parties the privilege of shooting their own personal weapons. There is no better way of being introduced to the shooting sports than to mingle with veteran shooters at the firing range, and veteran shooters want to see their protégé matched with a firearm which is perfect for their intended use. Veteran shooters will often have surplus holsters or other apparatus they are willing to sell for a fraction of the cost of purchasing new equipment. The National Rifle Association has a listing of all clubs and organizations which are affiliated or sanctioned by the NRA,[18] and the internet is an excellent place to begin a search for organizations in your community.

Once a novice shooter has decided on the specific firearm and carry system method which best suits their particular needs, the time to actually make the purchase of a firearm has arrived. When the new shooter is ready to buy a handgun, they would do well to remember one very important thing; "***inexpensive***" and "***cheap***" are not necessarily synonymous when referring to the quality and reliability of firearms. There are some excellent quality firearms on the market which carry relatively inexpensive price tags, and the sale price of any particular pistol can vary greatly between the different retailers. That said, the shooter needs to understand that there are distinct advantages in purchasing their firearms through a local retailer; aka the neighborhood gun store. Most of the local retailers will stand behind the products they sell, and can assist the shooter by offering their continued help after the sale has been made. They can often serve as an intermediary between the manufacturer and the consumer. This is particularly true of the dealers who have been in business for a substantial amount of time. They are embedded members of their community. This in itself, is a valuable element of the purchase, and should be considered when choosing the best place to buy a particular brand and model of handgun. National retailers may offer an attractive discount, yes, but they cannot offer the same after-sale partnership and hands-on assistance that the neighborhood gun dealer can... at least in most circumstances. They have an obvious interest in making their customers happy; in that a happy customer will perhaps be a repeat customer. They are also well-seasoned in assisting their customers through the required reporting and the necessary paperwork which is mandatory in the purchase of all firearms.

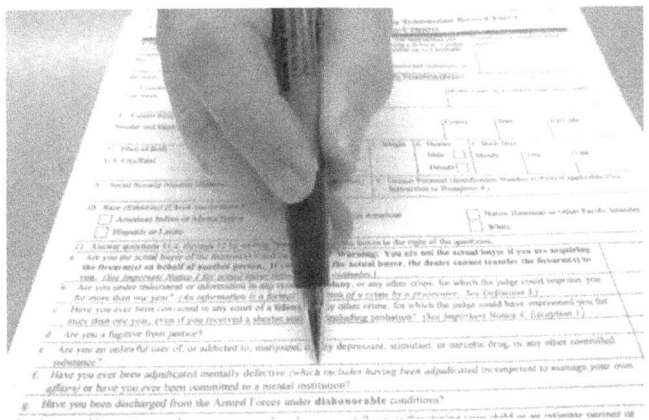

The Federal Government requires that a form 4473 be completed for all FFL sales

At the time that the sale of a firearm is made, and before the buyer can take legal possession of their new firearm, there are documents to be filled out in order to comply with the federal government's mandated regulations (Bureau of Alcohol, Tobacco, and Firearms, or ATF). Form 4473 needs to be executed. In a nutshell, form 4473 requires that you show proper identification to the Federal Firearm Licensed (FFL) merchant from whom you are buying the firearm. This identification must be an official picture ID, such as a driver's license or passport. On this 4473 form, you must indicate under oath that you are not a felon, you are a citizen of the United States, and you have not been convicted of any crime or crimes (even some misdemeanors) which would prohibit you from owning a firearm. Your identification must also verify the fact that you reside in the state in which you are purchasing the firearm. Once the form has been completed, your name and personal statistics are run through the national database of the Bureau of Alcohol, Tobacco, and Firearms in Washington, D.C. (*this is usually performed via telephone call from the retail vendor to the ATF purchase hotline, or in some cases, directly over the internet*). Once the ATF has approved the sale (*usually just a matter of only a minute or two*), the retail merchant will be given a transaction approval serial number which he or she will enter on the 4473 form, and the sale is then considered sanctioned, approved, and complete. The dealer retains their copy of form 4473 for their own records in the event they are audited by the ATF, and the purchaser is then free to leave the store with their new firearm in their possession. (*In some states and localities there is a waiting period before the buyer can actually take possession of a firearm*) When the ATF performs their random audits, the dealer must have a properly executed 4473 form on file for every firearm sale they have made.

Note: Effective January 16, 2017, the Bureau of ATF has revised form 4473 to include two additional questions

There's a lot more to consider when buying a handgun than just the price tag, and not every handgun is suited for concealment

Choosing An Appropriate Firearm

As mentioned in the previous pages, "*cheap*," and "*inexpensive*" are not necessarily synonymous when it comes to the purchase of a reliable firearm, or firearm related equipment. Since the practice of concealed carry has become so popular, firearms manufacturers have introduced a vast array of new weapons and paraphernalia designed and engineered specifically with concealment in mind, and many of these newer styled, polymer-framed, semi-automatic and revolver firearms are very affordable. Statistics show that infallibly, the most popular caliber over the years among concealed

101

carriers has been the .38 caliber in revolvers, and the 9 millimeter Luger (9X19) in the semi-automatic pistols. The German firm of Deutsches, Waffen, und Munitionsfabriken of Berlin, (German Arms and Ammunition Factory) developed and introduced the 9X19 cartridge (*known then as the 9mm Parabellum*) in 1902. Little did they know at the time that a century later their progeny was to become the most widely used service pistol cartridge in the world by law enforcement personnel, and there are good reasons for the cartridge's immense popularity. It is a cartridge capable of being fired from a relatively small-framed and lightweight pistol, yet it packs enough punch to gain the respect of ballistic experts and firearm enthusiasts as well. Although many law enforcement officers have opted to use the .45 ACP, and more recently the .40 caliber Smith & Wesson as their caliber of choice for their service weapons,[19] the majority of law enforcement officers today still prefer to carry the 9mm Parabellum, (or 9x19) when on duty.

In 1908, the American firm of Colt Manufacturing Co., Inc., introduced the similar but noticeably smaller .380 (*Automatic Colt Pistol*) cartridge, which was capable of being fired from an even smaller weapon, thus making handguns even easier yet to conceal. Although there are many other calibers used in pistols, revolvers as well as semi-automatics, the 9mm Luger and the .380 ACP are by far the most popular among concealed carry enthusiasts today. The .32 ACP (Automatic Colt Pistol), also known as the .32 Automatic is a centerfire pistol cartridge. It was introduced in 1899 by Fabrique Nationale, and is also known as the 7.65×17mm SR Browning, or 7.65 mm Browning Short. The .32 S&W cartridge was introduced in 1878 to be used especially for the Smith & Wesson Model 1½ revolver, a handgun conceived and designed specifically for concealment. It was originally engineered as a black powder cartridge. The .32 S&W was offered to the public as a light, defense cartridge, for what they called "*card table*" disputes, and also known as a "*gentleman's vest pocket pistol.*" As improved cartridges were being introduced, the popularity of the .32 faded, as the cartridge failed to have the ballistic "*knock down power*" of the .38 caliber revolvers or the .380 and 9mm semi-automatics. Many experts claim that the .38 Smith & Wesson revolver has been the single most popular handgun carried in America for the last fifty years, and despite all of the concealed carry models available on the market today, the Smith & Wesson small and medium framed .38 has retained its '*number one*" status.

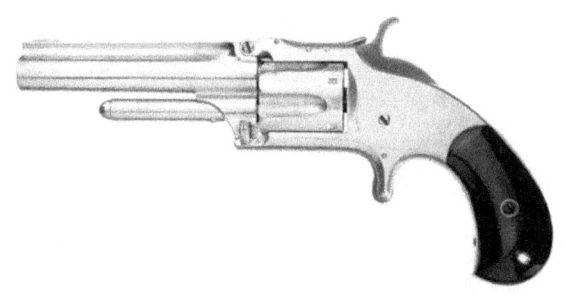

Smith & Wesson's Model 1½ revolver, circa 1878

The Smith & Wesson Model 60 – among the most popular concealed handgun in America for over fifty years

Just like their .32 caliber predecessor, the .380 pistols of today come in many makes and models which are small enough to be considered *"pocket pistols,"* meaning they generally fit well and can be carried in a purse, coat, or vest pocket.   Be aware, however, that there are a large number of law enforcement professionals who are of the opinion that the .380 cartridge is a caliber which is insufficient to carry as a defensive weapon – that the impact of the .380 bullet lacks the power to immediately disable and stop an aggressor. That doesn't mean that the .380 is worthless as a defense caliber, it simply means that in the opinion of many professionals, there are other calibers which are more effective against aggressors.

It should also be noted that Ruger made a significant contribution which competed with Smith & Wesson and Colt in the area of service revolvers, when they introduced the classic Service-Six and Speed-Six in 1972. These revolvers were manufactured through 1988, and are highly sought after among shooting enthusiasts. Chambered in .357 Magnum as well as the .38 Special, they became the carry weapon of many state policemen throughout the United States, and are still carried by some law enforcement personnel today.

The Classic Ruger Speed-Six in .357 Magnum

Before actually selecting a brand and model of handgun to purchase, it would be time well spent to familiarize oneself with the reviews of the different firearms which have been posted on the internet. There are some firearms on the market today that carry a history of inferior and unreliable performance, but are otherwise attractive because of their lower price. No amount of savings could possibly justify the purchase of an unreliable handgun – period! Your life and the lives of your family should not be put at risk for the selfish purpose of saving a few dollars. However, it has been stated previously that "***inexpensive***" and "***cheap***" are not necessarily synonymous when it comes to the selection of a reliable handgun. Here again, the reviews of gun owners and firearm experts can be an invaluable source of information when trying to decide on the most appropriate handgun and caliber. Some semi-automatic handguns function flawlessly when they are firing a certain type of ammunition, but are prone to jam occasionally when shooting some other types of ammunition. Some brands and models of handguns have a history of functioning with limited failures regardless of what types of ammunition are used.

A very close friend and his wife went with me and my wife to the firing range last year. He had just purchased a brand new 9mm semi-automatic carry gun for his wife at the astonishing low price of $175. As she was running the first magazine of ammo through the gun it exploded in her hand. Thankfully, she escaped any injury, but parts of the gun were lost when they flew into oblivion. For a moment, imagine something like that happening during a time of serious confrontation with an armed aggressor, and then consider the so-called "***savings***" which amounted to about two hundred dollars. The handgun in question carried a lifetime warranty from the manufacturer, and the weapon was sent off, repaired, and returned – supposedly reliable now. Here again, think about what the episode must have done to their confidence in the dependability of that particular firearm. The handgun in question will probably function perfectly forever now that it has been repaired – yet that one incident of failure has planted the seed of doubt. Today, she carries a different handgun for her personal protection, and in my opinion, for good reason.

One of the less expensive semi-automatic handguns on the market today is manufactured in Argentina and sells for considerably less than $400.[7] The reviews and field tests on this particular handgun are extremely favorable, even outstanding, so I purchased one in the .45ACP caliber (my preferred carry caliber). I have now shot several hundred rounds through the gun and have never experienced a failure of any type, regardless of the variety of cheap ammunition I have used. Models which are comparable in the quality of workmanship and history of reliability are available from other more popular American manufacturers. These guns retail for between $600 and $750 and even more. Yet I couldn't be more pleased or have more confidence in the reliability of my Argentinian choice. In my humble opinion, the handguns that are available from this particular manufacturer represent the best values in handguns on the market today. Yet for some unknown reason, gun enthusiast buyers tend to prefer the higher priced comparable handguns. I mention this in order to reiterate – cost and quality can vary greatly in firearms, and cost is not necessarily an indicator of quality. Do your homework and study the reviews and field tests – you'll be glad you did.

The following considerations should be given due thought before actually purchasing a handgun:

1) Does the gun feel comfortable in my hand?
2) Does the weight of this gun make it burdensome to carry?
3) Are there features of the gun which could possibly snag on my clothing when drawing it?
4) Does it feel as though it points naturally toward the target when it is held?

When deciding which caliber of handgun would be the best selection for you, there are trade-offs that should be considered. Law enforcement personnel as well as ballistic experts will generally agree that when a .45 caliber bullet strikes an assailant's body, the impact is so shocking that the person is likely to be disabled by even a wounding shot, such as a shoulder, leg, or arm. The weight of the bullets alone can be dramatically different. For example, the weight of an average 9mm bullet is most commonly in the range of 115 grains, or 0.263 ounces, and the weight of the most common .45 caliber bullets usually averages 230 grains, or 0.526 ounces – twice the size and weight, so one can logically assume that the .45 caliber bullet has twice the stopping power. From a standpoint of disablement, this fact alone makes the .45 caliber the most attractive in its potential of quickly putting an armed assailant out of commission. The 9mm and the .45ACP have notably different muzzle velocities (the 9mm averaging 1,100 foot pounds and the .45ACP about 900). In order to provide an "*over-simplified*" explanation of the difference in the two calibers, you can think of it in terms of colliding in a head on collision with a Volkswagen, versus a dump truck. I'm sure that there are more technically appropriate explanations from a ballistic standpoint if you care to research the subject, but because of its subjective nature, that's not something I care about addressing here. Suffice to say, the .45ACP delivers much more energy upon impact.

When we look at the handguns that are available in the .45 caliber the trade-off is obvious; most .45 caliber handguns require larger and heavier frames and slides which are necessary to handle the larger load, and these heavier firearms can weigh substantially more than some of the smaller 9mm or .380ACP handguns. However, with concealment in mind, in recent years manufacturers have scaled down the size of some of their .45 caliber model handguns, introducing compact and even sub-compact versions of their full-sized brothers. There are even scaled down versions of the famed 1911 Colt frames. But along with these lighter and smaller models comes increased hand shock and recoil to the shooter, adding to the difficulty of selecting the handgun and caliber that best suits the needs of the person who will be carrying the weapon. I mention this to bring emphasis to the fact that there are many things to consider when selecting a specific handgun and caliber to be carried on your person. Each of us are different; our sensitivity to recoil, our comfort zone and physical ability to carry larger handguns, and our specific likes and dislikes from an aesthetic point of view. If we all had the same needs and the same likes and dislikes, there would only be a need for one model handgun to meet the needs of everyone, and only one caliber of bullet available to shooters.

Unless a person was independently wealthy, a great deal of cost could be incurred unless forethought and research was used in making a handgun purchase decision. If a person who is interested in becoming a concealed weapon carrier takes their time and utilizes resources such as the internet, flea markets, gun shows, and classified ads, they can avoid the high cost of making that initial step into firearm ownership as well as the realm of concealed carry. Firearms are often purchased to serve specific purposes, and concealed carry consumers are a good example because they are outfitting themselves to serve a specific purpose; reliable concealed personal defense.

If you are one of those veteran gun enthusiasts who happen to own a number of different handguns that are appropriate for concealed carry and often find yourself wondering which weapon you should carry on any given day, you might want to try an experiment which has proved useful for me. First, weigh each of your handguns to determine their mass weight when fully loaded. In my case, I assigned a point value; with the lightest gun receiving the highest point value in that category. You might also consider assigning a point value based on the gun's ergonomics and how well you can shoot that particular handgun; this is subjective, I know, but in reality it's important enough that it should be taken into consideration. Next, determine a point value for the caliber of each handgun – with the higher caliber receiving the highest points. For example, a .45ACP caliber would rate much higher than that of a .380ACP simply because of its superiority in shock upon impact. Then, assign a point value based on the capacity of rounds carried by each handgun. Finally, determine a point value for each handgun's concealability – with the highest points going to those handguns which are the easiest and most effective to conceal. When you are finished, you should be able to add up each handgun's total points to see which ones score the highest. You might be surprised by the results. However, seasoned firearms carriers and ballistic experts would likely declare such an assessment unscientific and extremely subjective, and perhaps they would be right. It does, however, bring us closer to understanding the depth of our effectiveness as concealed carriers – that in itself might make this exercise well worth the effort. Here again, if we own multiple handguns, it only makes sense that we should carry the one(s) which are the most effective, and provide us with the most comfort and confidence.

In the two pictures which follow, I make a weight comparison between two of my concealed carry firearms. The difference in mass weight amounts to a pound – it doesn't sound like much, but in fact, it's a remarkable contrast.

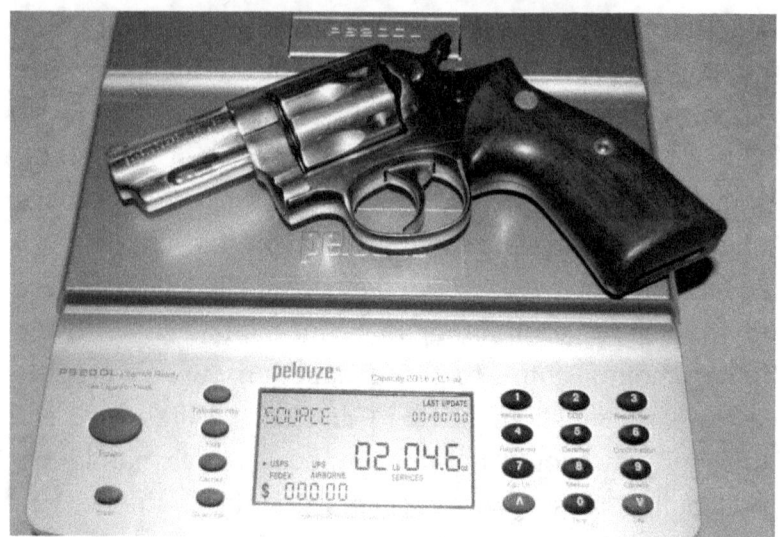

My Ruger Speed-Six .357 mag. weighs in at 2 pounds, 4 ounces

My 9mm Sig Sauer P-938 weighs almost precisely a pound less

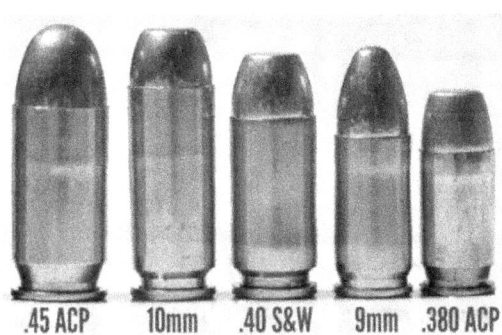

.45 ACP   10mm   .40 S&W   9mm   .380 ACP

The most popular calibers in semi-automatic handguns today

There is such a large variety of handguns on the market today that it can be very confusing for a person to determine exactly which handgun is going to be the best for them, and suit their specific needs the best.

The large variety of semi-automatic handguns on the market today can lend confusion to selecting the right one for you

In the years following its development, the .380 ACP cartridge came very close to dying an obscure death during the mid-twentieth century, save for the fact that the caliber became immensely popular in Europe, particularly during the 1960's and 1970's. In recent years its popularity in America has soared – especially in light of the fact that it is such a perfect caliber for smaller and easier to conceal pistols. Nevertheless, the .45ACP, .40 S&W, 9mm Luger, and the .380 ACP undeniably remain as the most popular calibers in semi-automatic handguns today. In revolvers, the .44 magnum, .357 magnum, and .38 Special remain the favorites. Yet it's wise to remember that not every caliber nor every handgun are suited for the needs of every shooter. Some calibers can produce a heavy *"kick,"* or recoil when fired. The discomfort produced by these recoils can be painfully disturbing to some shooters, while others pay it no mind. However, if recoil causes a shooter to practice their shooting less often, they should be advised to purchase a handgun caliber with which they are comfortable. If they shoot less often, it only figures that they will be less proficient overall, and also less familiar with their handgun. Therefore, a shooter (or concealed weapon carrier) needs to choose a caliber and a weapon which they are comfortable in shooting. Once again, there can be no better way of deciding on the right handgun than to visit your local retailer as well as your nearest shooting range. It's certainly more cost effective to make the appropriate selections the first time, when purchasing your initial firearm. In respect to resale value, most modern handguns are not unlike used cars, in that their market value decreases the moment the car is driven off the dealer's lot. Before buying, research is time well spent.

Manufacturers have introduced scaled down versions of the .45 caliber handgun which can be carried comfortably

Feminine shooters, or younger shooters, and men with smaller hands might be well-advised to select the .380 or the 9mm as their carry caliber of choice. The recoil is minimal from these calibers, and the smaller pistol size makes it easy to conceal one in a purse or a fanny pack and is also more comfortable to hold for shooters with smaller hands. With the .380 ACP having become such a popular choice among concealed carriers, some manufacturers of ammunition now offer "*beefed-up*" versions of the .380 ACP cartridge which possess a greater velocity and slightly heavier projectile weight, resulting in a greatly increased shock upon impact.

During the late 1960's and throughout the 1970's, many of the smaller European handguns did not meet the import criteria of the 1968 Gun Control Act[15] due to their small size. Imported weapons had to meet specific minimum size requirements in order to qualify to be brought into the USA. This is regretful, for many of the smaller European handguns produced during that time were absolute works of art and craftsmanship; precision shooting instruments of outstanding quality. And speaking of quality, a potential buyer should be aware of the fact that all handguns do not have to look like something Batman would carry; i.e., finished in a flat-black and tactical motif... a more or less combat-utility theme. It's perfectly acceptable for a person to consider a handgun as being a precision instrument crafted as a work of art, whose beauty and craftsmanship are to be admired. We've been overly programmed here of late that "*only tactical is practical*," and handguns should all have lasers, flashlights, and other accessories attached. I'll buy that to some extent – especially in the case of law enforcement or other professionals. Their handguns are tools of their trade, with a definite menacing "*utility*" look about them. Yet I cannot help but feel that the '*military theme*' of some of the weapons manufactured today are to a great extent a fad that consumers are caught up in. I suppose that I'm rather archaic in that respect, because I appreciate those occasions in which I can sit quietly in my easy chair and fondle some of the features of the finer craftsmanship in some of my handguns. In my hands, and under an admiring eye, I can study the detail and beauty of a firearm that is ascetically pleasing to me in appearance, machined to exacting tolerances, and complimented by grips that lend distinction and an air of personality and character to the weapon. That's just the way it is with me, and I can appreciate the fact that not everyone feels that way. Some guns are more than just guns to me – they can be a work of art, a tangible link to the history of our great nation, a product which represents our freedom as a nation and also represents our physical ability to exercise our Second Amendment rights.   The point that I'm trying to make is that a newcomer should be advised that there is beauty in deeply blued and finely machined steel, and in stainless steel and nickel.   Every gun does not have to be half plastic, have a laser gizmo attached to it, jet-black in color, and have black rubber grips. I'm not trying to push the nickel-plated, gold-triggered, and pearl-handled handguns here, *(Gen. George Patton would have called them "pimp" guns)* I'm simply suggesting that there are appearance options available other than *"SWAT-TEAM"* black, or *"doomsday"* grey. Undoubtedly, *'Rambo'* and Arnold Schwarzenegger would disagree with me here, but I can't help feeling the way I feel about the more traditional handguns.   A man cannot spend nearly seventy years of his life growing up with traditional firearms, and suddenly fall in love overnight with something that looks like a *'Star Wars'* toy.   Now that

I've got that off my chest, I'll climb down from my soapbox so we can move on.

As has already been mentioned previously, for most of us, price can be another mighty important consideration, and in that respect, it can pay a potential buyer to shop around before they rush out and purchase the first handgun they find. Most firearms manufacturers publish a suggested retail price in the advertisements for their products (Manufacturer Suggested Retail Price, or '***MSRP***'). These prices are exactly what they imply – "***a suggested price***," and the actual retail cost or sale price that a consumer has to pay at time of purchase can sometimes be substantially lower than the listed *MSRP*. Case in point: As an example, a specific Smith & Wesson semi-automatic pistol in the 9mm caliber has a MSRP of $549.00, but the actual retail price at the neighborhood gun store can be as low as $449.00 (sale priced at $394.95 by a national sporting goods chain store). The same model of '*used*' gun can be purchased in excellent condition for about $300.00* if you shop around or visit a gun show. (*State and local taxes can apply, as well as transfer fees and possible shipping fees charged by the dealer in some cases.)

When choosing between a revolver and a semi-automatic pistol, there are again several things to be taken into consideration. A revolver is much simpler to use and maintain, and with few exceptions, a revolver commonly has fewer safety concerns. But generally speaking, with the exception of the light-weight models, revolvers can sometimes weigh substantially more than their semi-automatic counterparts that have an alloy or polymer frame. Revolvers can also have a smaller capacity for ammunition than some of the polymer frame semi-automatics. Most center-fire revolvers have a round limitation of five or six in a rotating cylinder, while some of the compact semi-automatic polymer pistols can hold as many as ten rounds or more in their magazine. Your licensed firearms dealer will be glad to show you the differences in the two, explain the advantages and disadvantages, and assist you in making the selection that is right for you. It is also worthy to mention the fact that when the larger magazines are filled with extra rounds, they can add substantial weight to a handgun. This is a fact which merits consideration by a concealed carrier. When loaded to capacity, the magazine alone of one of my semi-automatic handguns weighs 10.2 ounces, and together with the weight of the handgun totals 2 pounds, 8.6 ounces, or nearly twice the desirable weight of an ideal firearm which can be carried comfortably.

Size comparison of the full-sized, sub-compact, and the micro

After having paid so much tribute to the semi-automatic handguns, I hesitate to leave this section without first giving the revolver its due mention. Revolvers have served concealed weapon carriers quite capably for more than a century, and there are a variety of good, dependable revolvers on the market today. Manufacturers such as Colt, Taurus, Ruger, and Smith & Wesson continue to provide quality concealed carry firearms to fill this niche. Many firearms enthusiasts and firearms experts have rated the J-Frame Smith & Wesson models as the single most popular concealed firearm in America today, and for several good reasons. With an alloy frame, and weighing in at just over fourteen ounces, and with a barrel length of only 1.87 inches, the models 442, 637, and 638 have an overall length of about six inches, making it very easy to conceal. In addition, these models come in the time-tested and dependable .357 Magnum or the .38 S&W Special caliber, making them highly desirable as a concealed weapon. Also to be considered, is the fact that revolvers are much easier to clean than their semi-automatic counterparts, and experts consider them much safer to carry and handle. When purchasing a firearm as a concealed carry weapon, the buyer owes it to themselves to at least consider the revolver before making a final decision.

Following the purchase of your concealed carry firearm, it's your responsibility to safely familiarize yourself with every aspect of the gun, including disassembly for cleaning, reassembly, routine maintenance, loading and unloading, as well as the use of any and all safety features which the gun might have, such as a thumb safety or palm safety. If you purchase a new gun, read the owner's manual that comes with your firearm thoroughly. If you purchase a used gun and do not have a manual, owner's manuals can be downloaded free of charge from the manufacturer's internet web site. It's also important that you record the serial number of your newly purchased firearm and keep it in a safe place for future reference. If the weapon is ever stolen, law enforcement will need the make, model, and serial number in order to file a theft report with the State Bureau of Investigation and the FBI. Serial numbers are located in two places on most handguns.

As mentioned already on page 27, put adequate planning into the place where you intend to store your firearm when at home. If there are children in the household, and you want to have your handgun readily accessible at your bedside during the night, there are a variety of bedside handgun safes available on the market today which can be quickly opened by an adult at a moment's notice. These types of safes render it impossible for a child to gain access to your handgun, offering great peace of mind to the firearm's owner. On many of these bedside safes, the numbers on the combinations of these safes are also in raised Braille, so they can easily be identified in the dark. It's wise to practice operating the safe's combination in the dark so you can be prepared for any eventuality, such as a power failure during a natural disaster or the extreme case of a home invasion.

The importance of firearm safety can never be over-stressed! It only takes one incident of carelessness or inattention to ruin lives.

Bedside safes can offer unparalleled firearm security

These bedside safes are quick and easy to open for an adult who knows the correct combination, yet virtually impossible for an adolescent to tinker with until it opens. It's another measure of firearm security which assures the safety of our children, and several models are available from retailers which can be purchased for under $200. Trigger locks are also available for all handguns, but they require the use of a key, and are cumbersome and time-consuming to open, especially during the time and confusion of an emergency. All new handguns sold in the USA today come with some fashion of trigger or other anti-operational lock as well as a padlock and two keys. Using the second hand on my watch, I once timed a friend of mine as he raised up in his bed and retrieved his handgun from a bedside safe. The total elapsed time that it took him to go from a sleeping position to retrieving his handgun and being in a mode that was considered armed and ready, was a mere thirteen seconds, yet the combination lock on his handgun safe rendered it completely safe from the tampering fingers of curious children.

Most bedside handgun safes can be bolted securely to the floor or furniture, and they also come in versions which are considered portable, and can be carried along on family trips, vacations, etc. Many of the models which are intended to be permanently mounted are aesthetically pleasing to the eye, and do not detract from the décor of the room. Even if they were a distraction to the eye, the security they offer makes them well-worth any sort of menial distraction.

Several configurations of gun locks are available, and each of them are effective in preventing children from having access to a loaded and functioning firearm

Storing loaded handguns in an unlocked drawer in a home where children live or visit is unacceptable

Bedside gun safes offer security as well as immediate access

Sleeping with a handgun tucked under your pillow or storing your firearms in a place where they are accessible to children is completely unacceptable. Accidents don't just happen – they occur when oversight takes precedence over prudence and good common sense, and we throw caution to the wind. I can't begin to imagine how hard it would be for a parent to live with themselves if they were to lose a child because of their own negligence and inattention to safety.

In the final analysis, when considering the purchase of a handgun for personal defense, these general factors should be considered in your selection:

1)   Plinking at the firing range is one thing – personal defense is something altogether different.

2)   Rapid deployment, accuracy, and the effectiveness of disablement are of extreme importance.

3)   If the weapon is to be carried, consider how effectively it can be concealed.

Once you have obtained your handgun, shoot it as often as possible.

Choosing An Effective Ammunition

With the many varieties and manufacturers of ammunition that the consumer has available to them today, few people would disagree that the quality of modern ammunition available on the market today (with some exceptions) is far superior to that which was available to shooters twenty or twenty-five years ago. There is even '*specialty*' ammunition available on the market today as well – ammunition which has been engineered and designed specifically for its increased shock and '*knock-down*' capability.   To   see   the devastating effects of some of the specialty ammunition, you can view the many videos on the internet which show the various ammunitions as they are fired into a block of ballistic gel. There is also a wide variety of "*economy*" ammunition available from retailers which can be utilized to make practice shooting less expensive. I'm no ballistic expert, nor do I pretend to be, but one only has to study the pages of sporting catalogs to see the vast array of ammunition available today. Having such a large selection to choose from can be confusing to the novice shooter or newcomer to concealed carry, so I've enlisted the help of people who are far more knowledgeable in the field of ballistics than I to assist me in addressing the subject here.

When it comes to ammunition that is to be used for self-defense, I'm not going to try to mince words here, the goal is to disable and potentially kill an armed assailant or opponent as quickly as possible – to neutralize the danger of the situation – with the hopes that your assailant will not have the opportunity to do the same thing to you or anyone else. That's a rather raw and unabashed summarization of our objective during an armed confrontation, but I feel a need to be candid here while we are discussing the subject of ammunition selection. Real life gunfights are nothing like those we saw on television when we were youngsters – when the Lone Ranger shoots the gun out of the bad guy's hand and marches him merrily off to jail. A gunfight is a gut-level life and death struggle that can happen in the blink of an eye, leaving carnage and death in its wake. That's not a very pretty picture, I know, but that's simply the way that events unfold in a real life and death situation. With that in mind, let's set our petty squeamishness aside for a moment and take a closer look at some of the ammunition available in today's marketplace. Some of the newer and more modern defense ammunitions have monikers such as, *"Critical Defense, Expanding Hollow-Points, and Extreme Handgun,"* and offer an increased knockdown power and expanding bullets which are designed to do the maximum damage to a target. Gunfights are not a game of chivalry, they are a sincere life and death contest from which one party walks away and the other party is carried away... hopefully the bad guy. Unfortunately, sometimes, both parties are carried away. Again, this is not a very pretty picture, it's simply the way things are in real life.

With that in mind, when choosing ammunition for your personal defense weapon, you will want the ammo which provides you with the highest odds of survival by disabling your assailant as quickly as possible. Don't be skittish, and don't try to save a nickel or dime here – buy something that will optimize your chances of surviving. If you must save money, do so when purchasing your practice ammo. This is another area in which your gun dealer can be a lot of help. When plinking at the practice range it's okay to buy inexpensive ammunition, it's even cost efficient to do so. But when loading your personal defense handgun to be carried on your person – to be used for the purpose of saving your life or possibly saving the lives of others, think like a survivor, not a miser.

Remember: A full metal jacket bullet (FMJ) will inflict less shock and damage to a target upon impact than a soft point, hollow point, or a bullet such as the ones which have been engineered and designed specifically for self-defense purposes. We are living in the age of candid videos, and the internet has a myriad of videos depicting real-life gunfights between the good guys and the bad guys. Many of these videos depict the bad guys firing several rounds at their opponents – even after they have been hit by what proved later to be a fatal gunshot. The smaller caliber FMJ projectiles may have proved fatal in the end, yes, but they lacked the severe initial impact which would have immediately disabled the aggressors – and actually afforded the aggressors an ample opportunity to return fire. As unpleasant as it might seem, this is a fact which must be taken into consideration when choosing appropriate ammunitions for your defensive carry handgun. Ask yourself this very important question:

Would you want your spouse to be armed with an ammunition in their defensive carry firearm which had been designed for target practice, plinking, or firing range use? I think not...

Once you have answered that question, and familiarized yourself with the available defensive ammo, make your choice for ammunition accordingly.

One of my favorite self-defense weapons is in the .357 magnum caliber. When practicing at the firing range, my .357 handguns will accept the less expensive .38 Special ammunition, taking a bite out of the high cost of shooting often, while maintaining my shooting skills. Likewise, there are retail outlets for ammunition which offer discounts for '*bulk*' purchases. A friend and I have periodically purchased a thousand rounds of 9mm and .38 Special ammunition at a greatly reduced bulk price, then split the purchase between us. It's generally not hard to find someone willing to go '*half's*' with you when it comes to buying ammunition.

CCW Reciprocity Within the USA and its Territories

(Current as of January, 2017)

Even within the states which permit licensed or unlicensed concealed and open carry, there are exceptions and limitations as to where a person is actually allowed to bring a firearm, as we discussed on pages *63* thru *68*. Store owners, property owners, or agents of these owners have the specific legal right to refuse having firearms brought onto their premises. Most Federal Government buildings as well as municipal courthouses, airports, schools, and county and state owned facilities also disallow firearms to be brought onto their premises. However, as we've already discussed, in most cases there are no penalties or fines imposed on a person who is discovered to be carrying firearms in these locations. Most of the time, the person is simply asked to leave. If you find yourself in such a circumstance, you would do well to quietly leave without causing a scene. Remember, in those cases while you are on their property the law is completely on their side, and they have the right to refuse your being there.

It is your responsibility to know and comply with all laws and regulations which apply to firearms if you intend to carry a concealed or openly carried weapon. When traveling to another state, failure to adhere to their laws could result in arrest and fines, as well as the confiscation and permanent loss of your weapon. Reciprocity might allow you to carry a concealed weapon in another state, but only if you abide by their regulations – and most states have little tolerance for those out-of-staters who are ignorant of their laws.

Following is a listing of states that currently honor the CCW Permits of other states, but be aware that CCW laws can change regularly. Before traveling, check the current laws in the state or states you plan to visit.

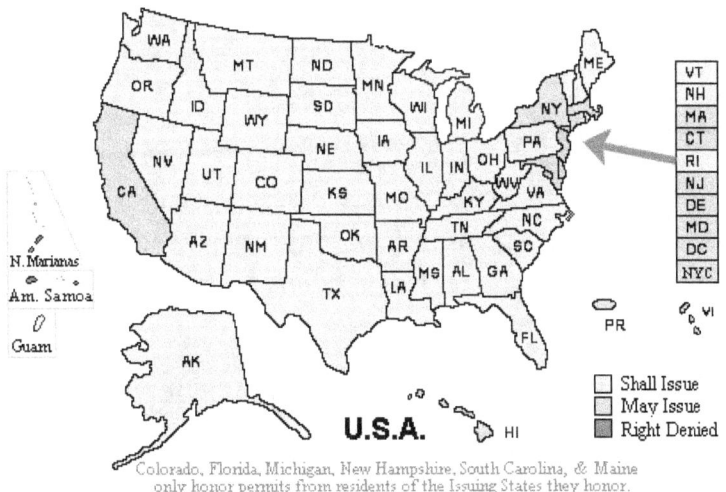

Colorado, Florida, Michigan, New Hampshire, South Carolina, & Maine only honor permits from residents of the Issuing States they honor.

AL, AK, AZ, AR, CA, CO, CT, DE, FL, GA, HI, ID, IL, IN, IA, KS, KY, LA, ME, MD, MA, MI, MN, MS, MO, MT, NE, NV, NH, NJ, NM, NY, NC, ND, OH, OK, OR, PA, RI, SC, SD, TN, TX, UT, VT, VA, WA, WV, WI, WY, and the District of Columbia all issue varying forms of CCW permits to their residents and honor permits that have been issued out of state.

Note:

Alaska, Colorado, Georgia, Guam, Kentucky, Louisiana, Michigan, Montana, Nebraska, New Mexico, Ohio, South Dakota, West Virginia, Wisconsin, and Wyoming will only issue new CCW permits to residents of their states.

Alabama, Arizona, Arkansas, Florida, Idaho, Illinois, Indiana, Iowa, Kansas, Maine, Minnesota, Mississippi,

Missouri, Nevada, New Hampshire, North Carolina, North Dakota, Oklahoma, Oregon, Pennsylvania, Puerto Rico, Rhode Island, South Carolina, Tennessee, Texas, Utah, Vermont, and Virginia will issue permits to their residents as well as residents of other states.

California, Delaware, New York City, and the Virgin Islands will issue concealed carry permits to their residents only.   In American Samoa and the North Mariana Islands, the right of citizens to bear concealed arms has been denied.

I would be remiss if I failed to comment on the gun laws of our nation's capital, Washington, D.C.   While our political leaders are protected by legions of heavily armed police, ordinary citizens of our nation's capital have been deprived of their rights by a cacophony of ridiculous laws and ordinances.   There is no better case to describe the outright absurdity of D.C.'s laws than to cite the case of a man who was convicted in 2014 for having a single inert dud shotgun shell and an empty .270 Winchester cartridge case in his home.   Residents of D.C. must register all rifles and shotguns with the Metropolitan Police Department, and ammunition can only be purchased legally for those particular firearms. There is no method of obtaining a handgun permit in Washington, D.C. or a concealed carry permit short of becoming a police officer.   Gun owners are advised to think twice before even passing through Washington, D.C., where a forgotten empty cartridge casing could lead to serious charges.   With 135 homicides in 2016, it is obvious that city lawmakers are wasting their bullets, so to speak, in their war against crime when they enact laws which have a negative impact on honest, law-abiding citizens.

On a brighter note, our current Presidential administration in Washington is advocating coast to coast reciprocity. In the meantime, we will have to wait to see if that actually happens. In the Senate, there will be much opposition to such a bill, especially from the states of California and Maryland.

Note: *This data and information has been gathered from sources posted on the internet as well as law enforcement personnel in the states of Oklahoma, Texas, and Virginia. It is currently correct information at the time this book went to press, however, be advised that these laws and regulations are subject to frequent change.*

Question:

"What am I to do if I am approached by a law enforcement officer while I am in possession of a legally carried concealed firearm?"

Do not start a conversation with any law enforcement officer by announcing, *"I've got a gun..."* **Do not attempt to retrieve or draw your handgun without the officer's explicit permission.** It is the consensus of a majority of concealed weapons carriers as well as the law enforcement officials I surveyed, that if you are stopped for a traffic check or a traffic violation, the officer will come to your vehicle and ask to see your driver's license and proof of insurance. When the officer asks for these documents, hand them your handgun permit along with your driver's license and proof of insurance. Keep both of your hands clearly visible to the officer, preferably at the top of the steering wheel of your vehicle. The officer will then ask if you have a firearm on your person or in your vehicle. You should answer politely in the affirmative; i.e., *"Yes, I have a holstered pistol on my right hip."* Or... *"Yes, I have a revolver in the center console of my car,"* or some similar response in order to advise the officer of the exact location of the weapon, as well as advise the officer that you are not trying to hide the fact that you're armed from him or her. **Do not panic**, because at this point the officer is most likely going to ask you to step out of the vehicle. For the officer's protection, he or she is likely to disarm you, and may or may not place you in handcuffs. Again, don't panic. They are doing this for his or her own protection, and as long as you are in compliance with the law, when the traffic stop is completed the officer will return your weapon to you and more times than not he will thank you for your honesty in declaring the possession of a handgun. And before you get huffy with the officer, put yourself in their shoes for a moment. They don't know you from Adam. Most of these officers are people with families at home, and they need to exercise extreme caution so that they can return safely to their families at the end of their shift.

Another possible encounter with law enforcement might occur when you are in public, when someone inadvertently catches a glimpse of your weapon when you reach for your wallet or checkbook. A spectator might become alarmed and place a call to 911 to report what they saw. If an officer is dispatched, chances are you'll be long gone and on your way well before the time an officer will arrive. If not, remain calm, answer any questions the officer might ask and show them your handgun permit when they ask to see it. Comply with their requests in a polite manner, and above all, **do not become irritated and angry. Anger is the quickest way to escalate the tension of a situation unnecessarily.** Remember, you are the one at fault in this circumstance for allowing your weapon to be seen by the public in the first place. Concealed carry means exactly what it says, "*concealed.*" The vast majority of police officers are in full agreement with an honest citizen's Second Amendment rights, they just need to assure themselves that you're not one of the bad guys – a felon, or a fugitive from justice, and that you are in compliance with the law. Unnecessary occurrences such as this should be a lesson to all concealed carriers to keep their weapons well hidden from the eyes of the general public at all times. The general public has been completely buffaloed by the news media's anti-gun hype – they are scared to death of guns, and they are even frightened by the honest citizens who carry them. Remember this, and don't do senseless things that will only add to the pandemonium.

In 2015, Michael Bryant, the sheriff of Jefferson County, Oklahoma, where I live, published an article in the newspaper in which he advised citizens to obtain a handgun permit and handgun if they did not already have one. This was a sincerely concerted effort to encourage citizens to have the means of protecting themselves, and a very responsible recommendation from the county's leading law enforcement representative at the time. Similar recommendations came from many law enforcement officials from across the nation, and such recommendations are indicative of the age in which we now live. The innocent, law-abiding public has endured more than its fair share of victimization in recent years, and the time for citizens to assume a more active role in their personal defense has arrived.

Maintaining Proficiency

As mentioned several times already, carrying a concealed weapon is an awesome responsibility. And it's a responsibility which should never be taken lightly. An important element of that responsibility is the ability to use your weapon efficiently and accurately in the event that a need should ever occur. The old adage, *"practice makes perfect"* applies profoundly to those individuals who have chosen to arm themselves. As carriers of concealed firearms we have an obligation to either keep ourselves acceptably proficient or keep our guns stored away at home in a safe place. Just as police officers are required to qualify periodically on the firing range, so should we practice frequently enough that we feel confident in our ability to protect ourselves and our families. That said, frequent practice is much easier for some folks than it is for others. Some people have the convenience of maintaining their proficiency at home, in a rural environment, and perhaps even right in their own back yard. In a more urban environment, some people have the fortune of living very close to a public or private firing range. For others, they might find it necessary to drive a long distance in order to find a suitable and safe place where they can practice often.

Regular practice is imperative for anyone who carries a permit for a concealed weapon

Our ability to practice regularly may also be impaired by a busy work or social schedule, or even restrictive health reasons. Nevertheless, we should practice as often as our individual lifestyles will permit.

When practicing, try to spend a little time safely simulating actual emergency conditions whenever possible. That is; draw your weapon safely and quickly, as if you were in a real life-threatening situation, and judge the accuracy of your first two or three shots. The overwhelming majority of gunfire situations occur within a distance of three to eleven yards. Hence, a good deal of your practice time should be performed at close range. Again, exercise extreme caution when practicing like this and don't allow yourself to get carried away. Bench shooting is both comfortable and enjoyable – I don't deny that. But during an emergency shooting situation it is more likely that you will be shooting freehand, from a standing position or a semi-standing, defensive position. That being the case, a portion of the time you spend at practice should be done under those types of conditions, and shooting from a defensive posture. After shooting frequently from this position you are certain to become more accurate and more comfortable in your stance. Remember: As a concealed carrier, the accuracy of your first three shots is the accuracy which is the most important, and those first shots are the ones which you should strive to improve and maintain. Be critical of yourself, but also keep safety as your number one priority as you practice. The benefits in this type of practice are twofold. Not only will your accuracy improve, the act of drawing your weapon will become more natural.

In a real-life situation, a person will be responding to an emergency without the benefit of hearing protection. But when practicing, it is absolutely essential that hearing protection is used.

It's also important to make your practice time as enjoyable as possible. It goes without saying that if your practice time is enjoyable, you will be more likely to practice often, thus improving and maintaining your proficiency.

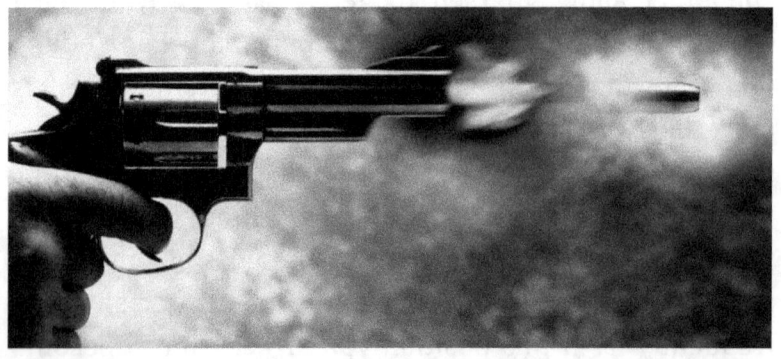

Whenever possible, try to practice occasionally under various shooting conditions. Even plinking with a small-caliber handgun can be an excellent way of honing your overall shooting abilities and keeping yourself proficient. Shooting at a target, such as a tin can or a pie plate while strolling through a woodlot, is also a good way to maintain your shooting form. Believe it or not, even shooting a BB-gun or pellet pistol as practice in your basement or garage – are excellent ways in which you can rehearse your shooting posture and keep your shooting eye keen.

If you have occasion to shoot with a friend or two, or perhaps your spouse, don't hesitate to critique one another, especially when it comes to handling your gun safely and maintaining the proper body position and shooting form; how the handgun is held, the position in which the finger is on the trigger, the position of the arms, or the common mistake of dropping the arm immediately after the shot – these are mistakes that are easy to make, and it can be of great help to have a partner who is willing to point out these errors – errors we might otherwise be overlooking.

While it may seem humorous that I would endorse practicing with a pellet gun or BB gun, you need to consider that some of the pellet guns on today's market are virtually indistinguishable from a real handgun, and they can be an excellent way to keep those marksmanship skills honed when there are no other viable practice opportunities available.

Pellet guns can look and feel very much like the real thing

Practice is one of those simple things that we must do in order to maintain a familiarity with our firearms. We may not realize it, but simply holding a handgun in our hands on occasion can stimulate those brain cells which keep us familiar with our weapon and what it feels like when we hold one in our hand. Whether you're on an official handgun range, in your own back yard, a woodlot or a friend's farm, practice as often as your time will permit – you'll find that its time well spent. Normally, I have to drive at least a half hour in order to visit a public firing range. However, recently a friend and I have set up a practice range in an obscure canyon on a neighbor's ranch, and I can now have unlimited practice opportunities five minutes from where I live.

As any new shooter will soon discover, shooting a handgun accurately isn't nearly as easy as they make it look on TV. Attaining proficiency requires a thorough understanding of the fundamentals of marksmanship coupled with a strong desire to improve. Because there are so many elements necessary to shoot well consistently, one of the best ways to better your skills is to analyze the shot placements on your targets routinely, and pay attention to what they're telling you.

Of the seven major fundamentals of marksmanship, sight alignment, sight picture and trigger control are the most critical elements in achieving and maintaining handgun accuracy. *"Sight alignment"* is the relationship between the handgun's front and rear sight. The *"sight picture"* is simply a matter of superimposing the aligned sights onto the intended target. *"Trigger control"* refers to the depression of the trigger to the rear until the handgun actually fires the shot.

To align your handgun's sights properly, you must confirm that the top of the front sight is level with the top of the rear sight. This ensures proper elevation, meaning that your aiming point is neither too high nor too low. Of course, you must also align the sights horizontally, keeping the front sight in the very center of the rear sight window. When your sights are aligned properly, there will be equal distance between the front sight and either side of the rear-sight window notch. If there is more of a gap on the right side, the pistol is pointing more to the left, and your shots will go that way, and vice versa.

Sight alignment becomes more critical as the distance between you and the target increases. Handguns Magazine field editor Dave Spaulding, founder of *Handgun Combatives*, and other experienced instructors will tell you that if your sight alignment is off by just 1/16th of an inch at 20 feet, the result will be at least a 4 ½ inch separation between the actual point of impact and your intended target.

How do you determine whether or not you're dealing with sight alignment issues? If, for example, your shots taken at the five-yard line are pretty tightly grouped, but at 20 yards they seem to be impacting considerably to the left, you may need to work on your sight alignment. However, it's a wise idea to also have someone else shoot the gun in order to rule out the possibility of the sights themselves being misaligned. If your sights are off, and/or your aiming point is off, the resulting misses will be even more dramatic at longer distances. Keep in mind, this scenario is only one possibility. These misplaced shots could also be an indication that the gun shifting in your hand as you shoot.

Analyzing a target is much like diagnosing a problem with an automobile.   A qualified mechanic can narrow the field of potential causes based on the way the vehicle is performing, just as you can eliminate certain shooting errors based on where your shots are impacting the target.   Finding the cure can sometimes be a frustrating exercise of trial and error, but finding the solution will certainly justify the time and effort.

As with most shooting problems, sight alignment can sometimes be improved dramatically through frequent *'dry-fire'* practice.[17]   With an unloaded handgun, simply focus and re-focus on your personal sight picture.   Then look for that proper placement of the front sight within the notch of the rear sight.   Rather than momentarily glimpsing your proper sight alignment, force yourself to stare at it for approximately 30 seconds at a time.   This will help you imbed the image of proper sight alignment into your mind so that it's easier for you to obtain when you're on the range or, more importantly, during a personal-defense situation.

Achieving a proper sight picture requires nothing more than placing those perfectly aligned sights over your intended target.   By combining proper sight alignment and sight picture, you have successfully aimed your handgun at your target.   As long as you maintain that proper aim throughout the process of firing your handgun, your point of impact should be very close to your point of aim—and the shot placements on your targets should reflect that.

If your points of impact are scattered, the problem could be that you're focusing more of your attention on the target than the front sight. As you can imagine, this is a serious concern when facing an armed assailant in the heat of a personal defense situation. In such confusion and turmoil, if your complete attention is focused on the threat, you're not focused on the front sight of your handgun.

For optimum accuracy, your attention should be focused attentively on the front sight at the time the trigger is actually depressed. This, of course means that both the target **and** your rear sight will be slightly blurred. That's okay... It's a condition that you will become accustomed to after practice. Many handgun shooters are aware of the importance of front-sight focus, but I wonder how many shooters are actually focused on the front sight at the exclusion of both the target and the rear sight.

It wasn't until I had carried a handgun for several years that I truly understood what it meant to obtain that elusive crystal clear image of the front sight. One day at the range, something finally *'registered'* in my mind, and the front sight became more pronounced than ever before. Prior to this revelation, I had merely looked at the front sight when shooting, but I hadn't focused on it as intently as was necessary to obtain the maximum accuracy from my handgun.

In order to emphasize the importance of front sight focus, many instructors have encouraged their students to look for a tiny imperfection on the front sight and focus on that as opposed to the entire front sight. You could also use a permanent marker or even fingernail polish to make a tiny dot on your front sight.

A mental refresher can be of use to some shooters: The shooter holds a pencil in their hand and extends his arm out in front of him/her. The shooter can pick a target in the distance and practice transferring his or her gaze from the tip of the pencil to the target and back again. This trains the shooter's eye to make the transition between the front sight and the target. It's important to remind the shooter that when the shot is actually fired, the focus should be on the tip of the front sight or, in the case of this practice session, the tip of the pencil.

Not even perfect sight alignment and sight picture can compensate for a lack of trigger control. In fact, trigger control is often cited as the most common error in shooting a handgun. The act of incorrectly depressing the trigger has been given many names. Since the index finger contracts during this process, many naturally refer to trigger manipulation as *'trigger pull.'* Regardless of what you choose to call it, correct depression of the trigger is vitally important. Most experts will agree that it's critical for the rearward movement of your index finger to be smooth and steady as it moves straight back to fire the pistol. Two of the most common trigger control problems are (1) to anticipate the gun's recoil— jerking the trigger—and (2) failing to move the trigger finger independent of the rest of the hand.

Anticipating recoil tends to result in a right- handed shooter's shots impacting low on the target. This phenomenon is readily apparent when you engage in dry-fire practice while using a pistol that is equipped with a laser. If, as a right-handed shooter, you jerk the trigger, the laser will slice downward and most likely somewhat to the left, showing you where your live rounds would have impacted.

Failing to move the trigger finger independent of the rest of the hand is less predictable because the point of impact is dependent on the movement of the shooter's hand when the trigger is activated. For instance if a right-handed shooter rotates his thumb clockwise during the depression of the trigger, his rounds are likely to impact to the right. This error is often referred to as *'thumbing.'* If your gun is the right size for your hand, you should be able to comfortably place the pad of your index finger (where your index fingerprint is located) on the trigger while maintaining a proper shooting grip with the bore in line with your forearm.

Too much finger on the trigger is likely to result in *'snatching'* the trigger, which will send a right-handed shooter's rounds to the right of his or her intended point of aim. This occurs because the distal joint bending reflexively causes the hand and muzzle to rotate clockwise. Too little finger on the trigger is known as *'pushing'* the trigger because it causes the trigger finger to push the trigger back and to the left as opposed to straight back, resulting in rounds impacting near the nine o'clock position on the intended target.

Another error associated with trigger control is called *'heeling,'* and occurs when the shooter exerts too much forward pressure with the heel of the hand as the weapon is fired. This will likely result in a shot group that is located near the 12 o'clock position on the target. Of course, this pattern could also be the result of an improper sight alignment, where the front sight protrudes above the rear sight. Again, target diagnosis, while extremely beneficial in narrowing down the field of potential shooting errors, is not an exact science.

Summarization Of Common Causes Of Handgun Inaccuracy

(1) SHOTS in Lower Left Quadrant:

This pattern is caused when the shooter jerks the trigger, causing the front-sight to dip low and to the left before the bullet leaves the barrel. To correct this type of error, the trigger must be slowly pressed until the shot fires, being careful while pressing not to disturb the sight alignment and sight-picture.

(2) SHOTS in 9 o'clock position:

This pattern is created when the shooter does not properly place the index finger on the trigger. In such cases, the shooter has a tendency to press the trigger at an angle instead of straight to the rear. This improper press causes the muzzle to shift to the left, with the shots striking in the 8:30 to 9:30 zone.

(3) SHOTS in Upper Left Quadrant:

This is caused by *'riding the recoil.'* This commonly occurs when the shooter anticipates the recoil and makes the handgun recoil before it really happens. This type of pattern can also be caused by improper follow-through. The shooter releases the trigger finger too soon and may flip the finger forward, causing the front-sight to rise to the left. Errors of this nature will usually produce shots in the 9:30 to 12 o'clock zone.

(4) SHOTS in Upper Right Quadrant:

Here the shooter has *'heeled'* the shots high on the target. This error is caused by anticipating the shot and, at the last moment before firing, giving the handgun a slight push with the heel of the hand. The front sight moves up to the right and the bullets strike the target in the 1 o'clock to 2:30 zone.

(5) SHOTS in the 3 o'clock position:

Here the shooter **'thumbs'** the handgun. Just as the shot begins, the shooter pushes the right thumb against the side of the frame, causing the aligned sights to move to the right.

(6) SHOTS in the Lower Right Quadrant:

This target illustrates what happens when a shooter's grip tightens as the trigger is pressed. This shot placement area can occur when the shooter's hand clamps or snatches at the last second. This movement causes the front sight to dip low and to the right, pushing the shots to the 3:30 to 5 o'clock zone.

(7) SHOTS directly below the point of aim:

The shot string in the 5 o'clock to 6:30 area is usually caused when the shooter **'breaks'** the wrist – another form of recoil anticipation. The shooter expects the handgun to recoil at a known instant and tries to fight or control this anticipated recoil by cocking the wrist downward. The shooter may mistakenly but subconsciously believe that the recoil can be lessened by holding the wrist down. This shot group can also be caused by a shooter who relaxes too soon.

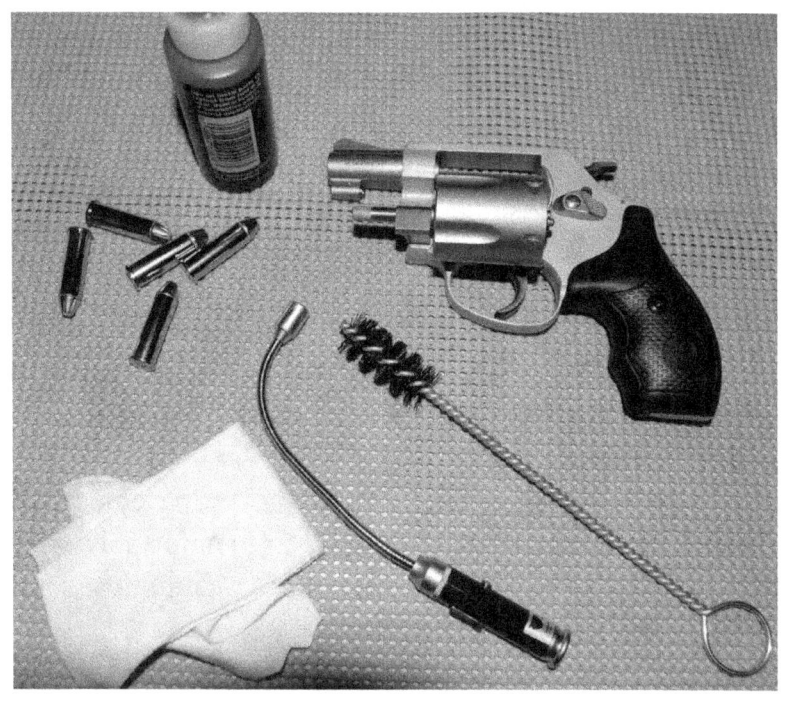

A Word About The Maintenance Of Our Firearms

Every firearms owner should know the importance of keeping their guns clean, lightly lubricated, and free of dirt and grime which can build up over a period of time and possibly cause the gun to malfunction. This is especially true of the semi-automatic handguns, as revolvers require much less in the way of maintenance. Keeping our firearms clean is one of the many responsibilities that are a part of gun ownership.

Everyone would agree that cleaning our guns is certainly not as enjoyable as shooting them, so it can be easy for us to overlook this very important chore, and possibly procrastinate one time too many. That being said, there are some things which can make firearms maintenance much less burdensome, and more convenient for us. Here are some of the things which have helped me:

1) First things first: always check and double-check to assure yourself that the firearm is unloaded – set any ammunition aside and well out of your way.

2) Establish a place in your home, basement, or workshop where you can comfortably and conveniently clean and maintain your firearms.

3) It should be a well-lighted place, and also a place which is off limits to children and toddlers – a place where you can concentrate, and give your full attention to the task at hand.

4) You should have everything you need within close reach; tools, cleaning cloths, solvent, and lubricants.

5) Be sure to remove any excess oil with a clean cloth. Once you have cleaned a particular firearm a few times, the sequence should become so routine that you could almost do it with your eyes closed.

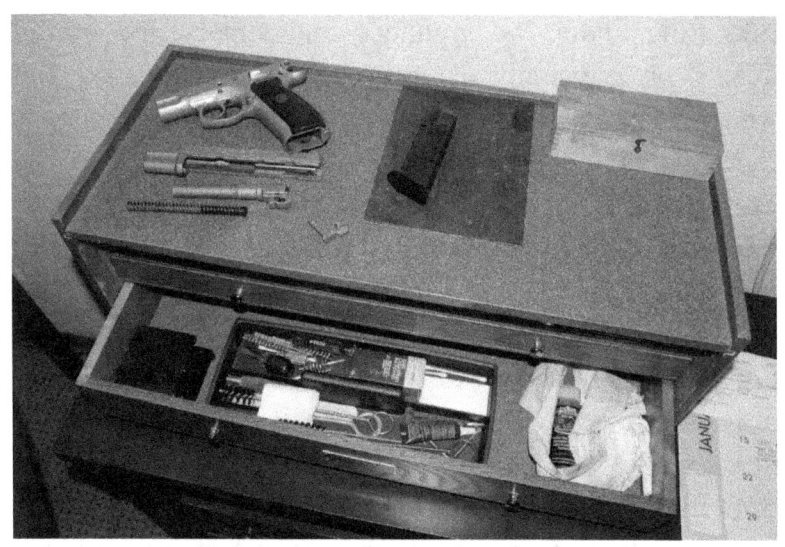

The author's firearm maintenance station

Revolvers are by far the simplest of handguns to clean, and in most cases do not require any type of major disassembly. For persons who are new to the process of cleaning their semi-automatic handguns, they should be forewarned that disassembly and reassembly of some brands of semi-automatic handguns can be a nightmare, especially until such time as the owner becomes accustomed to all the little secrets of that particular handgun. One of the *'higher profile'* manufacturers must assume that everyone has the *'finger-dexterity'* and coordination of a magician. It doesn't make any sense to me that they would engineer such fine firearms and yet be content with the frustrations they have created for their patrons. My advice to newcomers would be to perform this take-down and reassembly function for the first time under the guidance and supervision of the dealer or gunsmith from whom you purchased the weapon. In most cases involving semi-automatic pistols, there is a proper sequence of maneuvers to be performed, otherwise you can pull your hair out trying to figure out what you're doing wrong – this is especially true during the reassembly after cleaning. **Note: Trying to force components back together can cause permanent damage to the firearm and void the manufacturer's warranty**. If you feel a need to apply force in order to get things back together, you are doing something wrong. If the instruction manual is unclear, which many of them are, there are step-by-step videos available on the internet to assist you – both in disassembly and reassembly. Once you have uncovered the tricky little secrets and determined the proper sequence, practice disassembling and reassembling your handgun until you have acquired the proficiency to do so at ease. Some semi-automatic handguns are so simple to disassemble and reassemble that it causes you to wonder why some of the higher profile manufacturers haven't followed suit and engineered their models to be less of a nightmare to maintain. In my own humble experience, the semi-automatic handguns manufactured by Bersa and CZ-USA, are among the most foolproof to disassemble and clean. If you're going to depend on the gun, you should shoot the gun as often as possible. And accordingly, if you shoot the gun, it will require periodic cleaning. Why not choose a handgun that is '*user-friendly*' in this respect?

Semi-automatic handguns require disassembly in order to be cleaned properly

I cannot over stress the importance of keeping your firearms clean, properly lubricated, and in good, functional working order – this is an important item in the maintenance of all firearms, and especially important with semi-automatic firearms that are known to jam or misfire when grime, carbon, and dirt has been allowed to accumulate within the working mechanism. If there is any question in your mind regarding the importance of cleaning your firearm, take a close look at your cleaning cloth once you have finished. This is the carbon, dirt and grime that can build up over a period of time, harden, and cause your firearm to malfunction. Once you've finished the cleaning process, it's satisfying to know that your pistol or revolver is now free of dirt and ready to be taken to the range again or carried with confidence as your concealed carry weapon, clean and well lubricated.

Modifying Firearms

Personalizing firearms in order to make the weapon more attuned to the individual preferences of the shooter is a common practice. The installation of replacement grips or sights is often done in order to better suit the needs of an individual shooter. Replacement grips can make a great difference in how well the gun fits the shooter's hand. Beyond replacing factory grips or sights, when modifications are mechanical or internal in nature, such as tinkering with the inner components of a firearm, modifications should be performed by qualified gunsmiths only. Certain internal modifications may void the manufacturer's warranty. It's always a good idea to contact the manufacturer and seek their approval prior to making these types of modifications.

The Ineffectiveness Of Firearm Legislation

I doubt that legislative mandates have ever saved a single life when it comes to handguns, yet politicians have refused to learn from their past mistakes. One has only to look at the case of Jason Hamilton to see how ineffective legislation really is.

Jason Kenneth Hamilton had a lengthy rap sheet and a history of violent behavior that legally prohibited him from owning a firearm or carrying a concealed weapon in his home state of Idaho as well as anywhere else in America.

In 1991, at the age of 21, Hamilton was charged and convicted of domestic abuse. On various occasions in the years that followed, he was charged with aggravated assault, drug possession, pulling a gun on his landlord and threatening to "blow [his] *'f-in'* head off," and killing an ex-girlfriend's puppy whose back he broke after picking it up by its leash, choking, and kicking it. In June of 2006 he was convicted of domestic battery for strangling his live-in girlfriend until she passed out. The jury in the strangulation case wrote to the judge requesting the lengthiest sentence permissible by law.

The conviction very clearly prohibited Hamilton from legally owning firearms under federal law, but because of loopholes in federal and state gun laws, Hamilton was able to acquire several guns. And because of a weak permitting system in the state of Idaho, the "card-carrying Aryan Nations member" was even able to obtain a state permit to carry a concealed firearm.

Less than a year after his domestic violence conviction — and while holding his Idaho concealed carry permit — Hamilton went on a shooting rampage. He fatally shot his wife, and then set off for the courthouse where she had worked and fired numerous shots at the courthouse building. When law enforcement responded, Hamilton shot and killed a police officer. He then fled to a church across the street and, after shooting and killing the church sexton[16] there, he turned his gun on himself and committed suicide before he could answer for his crime.

Despite the continual debate over what legislative regulations are necessary in order to safeguard the general public from maniacs such as Hamilton, one fact looms ever-present in our social structure: Legislature is useless and ineffective unless the laws and regulations are enforced and criminals like Hamilton are effectively removed from society. When prison sentences amount to no more than the equivalent of going through a turnstile, then returning to society to resume a life of violence, any effectual degree of deterrence has effectively been eliminated from the criminal justice system. I cannot imagine how a judge or parole board could live with themselves after returning a career criminal like Hamilton to society, then learning that innocent lives had been lost as a result.

A robber armed with an AK-47 semi-automatic weapon stormed a Texas Waffle House, only to be shot by a legal concealed weapon carrying customer, police say. The suspect, who police believe to be 25 or 26 years old, entered the Waffle House restaurant in DeSoto, Texas and robbed the customers and business around 2:30 a.m. A concerned customer and licensed handgun holder told police that his wife was on her way to meet him at the establishment. Fearing that when she arrived the armed robber could harm her, he told police that he confronted the gunman in the parking lot.

When the suspect turned to face the armed customer with his rifle pointing in the customer's direction, the licensed handgun holder opened fire, shooting him several times, police said. The suspect was transported to a local hospital where he later died.

Police have publicly released photos showing some of the suspect's tattoos in a bid to potentially identify him, but to date, the assailant has never been identified. Police said the customer who shot the suspect was not arrested, nor was he charged in the shooting.

Sadly, incidents such as these are not isolated cases, or rarities in the world we live in today. News programs and newspapers are inundated with accounts of such violence on a daily basis – not because of the presence of guns in our society, but because of the number of deranged individuals who walk freely among us today – many of whom are on parole for having been convicted of other crimes. A rational-thinking citizen would assume that criminals on parole would have surely learned their lesson, and would now walk the straight and narrow so as to avoid a recurrence of encountering the criminal justice system again. Statistics show that not to be the case, and an alarming number of career criminals are returned to society each year.

On the same night, and at practically the same time that the gunman was robbing the Waffle Shop in DeSoto, Texas, twelve hundred miles to the northwest a much different scenario was unfolding. Twenty-six year-old Marjorie Whitcomb of Prescott, Arizona was traveling alone by automobile to visit her sister who lived in Billings, Montana. Near Cedar City, Utah, her car broke down at 2:00 AM, stranding her on route 15 in a remote area where she was unable to obtain a clear cell phone signal to phone for help. Two oilfield workers in a pick-up truck were returning to Archer City, Texas following a short term work assignment in Idaho and saw the woman on the opposite side of the highway. They promptly made a U-turn to go back to see if they could help. They tried to restart her car unsuccessfully. The men refused to leave Ms. Whitcomb in such a precarious situation in the middle of the night, and in such a remote location. They carried her into the town of Cedar City where they obtained a motel room for the woman and made arrangements for a local garage to tow the woman's car into town. The following day, Ms. Whitcomb's car was repaired and she was on her way once more to see her sister – thanks to the kindness of two men whom she had never seen before or since.

Had the wrong man, or wrong men happened upon her first, who knows what fate could have befallen the young woman? She was alone and vulnerable, although not quite as vulnerable as she might have appeared to an onlooker, and certainly not completely helpless. In the pocket of her jacket, she was carrying a 9mm semi-automatic pistol. Thankfully, because she was being assisted by honorable, good-intentioned men, she was never required to resort to its use. However, the two anonymous good Samaritans could have just as easily been men of ill intent. Marjorie Whitcomb would later say, "I don't know why, but I never felt threatened by these men. All they wanted was to help me get out of a difficult situation, and I thank God they came along when they did. I wish I knew their names and could thank them properly."

Needless to say, we are subject to meet honorable, well-intentioned people wherever we might go. They are not the reason we choose to carry arms for protection – we arm ourselves because of the ones who are not honorable or well-intentioned.

A Parting Word

I first started carrying a concealed weapon on my person while I was working in New York City in 1969 and 1970. I was once cornered in the basement of a downtown apartment building in Manhattan by two men who made it clear to me that they were intent on doing me harm. At first, they simply cursed at me, and tried to provoke me as I tried my best to ignore them. I suppose this frustrated them, so they became physical. I narrowly escaped up the basement stairway before a third man arrived, and I was so shaken by the close call that I made a vow to myself that I would never again be placed in such a vulnerable position – if I could help it. After that, I returned to the City more than two dozen times over the next four months, but I never returned to New York unarmed. Although I was never in a situation in which I had to draw my revolver, the feeling of safety made my subsequent trips to New York free from the pure terror of my previous vulnerability. The two thugs who had threatened me that day were striking union members of the same company that I worked for at the time. Even though I was a management employee, they accused me of being a scab (strikebreaker). They were arrested along with a third man a month later and charged with attacking and beating a sixty year-old AT&T management employee in Queens. The unfortunate victim remained in a New York hospital for two weeks before he was released to fly back to his home in Georgia. It could have just as easily happened to me, in fact, I'm convinced that if I had not been able to flee when I did, it would most assuredly have happened to me.

In those days there were very few hassles or legal red tape associated with carrying a gun. There were no x-ray devices at the airports, no searching of luggage (other than the thievery perpetrated by some of the airport baggage handlers), and no requirements for a person to have any sort of state-issued permit in order to carry a handgun. I had a letter in my billfold written and signed by a Virginia judge granting me his permission to be armed, and there was no expiration date on the letter. Things were much less complicated then, and the general public was not overly concerned that some people carried concealed weapons for their protection. I once took my jacket off when I got on the airplane shuttle to fly from Washington, DC to New York City and my Smith & Wesson .38 revolver fell out of my jacket pocket and onto the seat. (I did not own a holster at the time) The stewardess who was standing there smiled at me and said, "Excuse me, Sir, you dropped something..." Life was so much simpler then. There were no cell phones and no internet. When our plane would land at LaGuardia or Washington National, everyone would make a mad dash for a row of twenty or thirty pay telephones inside the terminal – so we could "*stay in touch*" with our business associates and families. Most of the criminal element in New York City practiced their violence against other criminal factions, and even on the streets of New York a private citizen was relatively safe when compared to today's meth-influenced criminal behavior on the streets. There was no *'crack heroin'* or methamphetamines, or at least none that I knew about or heard of. There were occasional newspaper accounts of muggings and other inner-city crimes, yet a person felt relatively safe, even on the streets of New York or Washington, D.C.

But as times change, so does the complexity of life's circumstances, and so must we. Carrying a concealed weapon is certainly not for everyone, and it's not my intention to suggest such a thing. It requires a personal conviction, mental discipline, and a keen awareness of the laws and regulations which govern that sort of thing. If there were no evil people in this world, such a thing as concealed carry would be unnecessary – law enforcement officers would not be needed, and the darkness of night would not bring the increased danger of the criminal element to the streets of the inner cities like a swarm of starving roaches.

If you are studying the possibility of carrying a concealed weapon on your person, give the matter its due consideration first and don't rush into the process. And if you decide in favor of carrying a weapon for your own protection, and for the protection of your family, may you be blessed to never have a need to resort to its use.

Whenever I pause long enough to look back at the span of my life, which has covered nearly three-quarters of a century, I try to contemplate the future of America with optimism. I have seen unimaginable medical advances which have enabled us to have much longer life-spans. These advancements have accounted for saving millions of lives each year, and for that I am thankful. Yet my optimism is displaced by anger whenever I'm confronted with the headlines which continuously depict the moral decay and criminal enterprises so omnipresent in today's high-tech world. The human addiction and dependence on electronics is probably not as destructive as I sometimes perceive it to be, but we as a people have been so inundated with technological advances that we seem to be losing touch with so many of the human aspects of life. We are rapidly wandering farther and farther away from the concepts which have united us and brought us together as the most powerful and wealthy people ever to occupy the face of our planet. But somewhere along the way we have developed an extremely unhealthy tolerance to criminal behavior – conveniently allowing attorneys to negotiate with criminals in the courtroom in an absurd ritual that we have come to call '*plea bargaining*.' We send lawbreakers away to correctional institutions where they can serve ridiculously short terms, and then we effectively turn our backs and allow parole boards to shorten those sentences even more, and in many cases our police officers on the street find themselves dealing with the same criminal element over and over again.

If we as a people would only take an intermission in our busy lives long enough to consider what attributes have initially brought us all of this prosperity, technological superiority, and affluence as a people united, we might be able to see through the haze and smoke of time well enough to realize that our unity as a nation, and our sovereignty as a people must surely be attributed to our Christian values and our dedication to one god above all. Without turning this into some kind of sermon, I'll simply say that when a people find it in their best interest to arm themselves before going from their homes into the public sector, something vitally important is lacking in the society in which they live. A change is in order, and I can think of no change that would be more beneficial to us as a people, than re-embracing those fundamental Christian values which sustained our forefathers, formed the foundation for our freedom, and brought us to where we are today. I can only pray that this will happen – but until it does, I will continue to keep myself armed whenever and wherever I deem it necessary. God bless and keep you and your family.

Resources

The National Rifle Association - 11250
Waples Mill Road, Fairfax, VA 22030. (800) 672-3888 +

National Association For Gun Rights - P.O.
Box 7002, Fredericksburg, VA 22404, (877) 405-4570
www.nationalgunrights.org

Guns & Ammo Magazine - PO Box 37539,
Boone, Iowa 50037-0539 United States 800-800-2666
www.gunsandammo.com

Gun Owners of America (GOA) – 1801 Forbes
Pl., Suite 102, Springfield, VA 22151 – PH: 703-321-8585
www.gunowners.org

National Shooting Sports Foundation
(NSSF) - 11 Mile Hill Road, Newtown, CT 06470
203-426-1320

United States Concealed Carry Assoc.
(USCCA) - Delta Defense, LLC, 300 S 6th Ave, West
Bend, WI 53095 1-877-677-1919

Citizens Committee For The Right To Keep And Bear Arms (CCRKBA) –
www.ccrkba.org   425-454-4911, toll free: 1-800-486-6963

National Association for Gun Rights -
National Association for Gun Rights, P.O. Box 7002, Fredericksburg, VA 22404 (877) 405-4570

The Crime Prevention Research Center -
Crime Prevention Research Center, 212 Lafayette Ave., Swarthmore, PA 19081 or... Crime Prevention Research Center, 3682 King Street, P.O. Box 3243, Alexandria, VA 22302

Bureau of Justice Statistics –
Bureau Of Justice Statistics, 810 Seventh Street, NW, Washington, DC 20531, 1-202-307-0765, bjs.gov

Firearms Policy Coalition –
4212 N. Freeway Blvd., Suite 6, Sacramento, CA 95834, 855-372-7522' www.firearmspolicy.org

There are enough pro-gun ownership organizations across America to make it confusing as to which groups would be the best and most effective in representing gun owner rights.   The lengthy list of organizations include, but are not limited to, such groups as *Gun Owners of Massachusetts, Gun Owners of California, The New York Gun Owners Association, the American Rifle Association (ARA), Well-Armed Women, LLC, Concealed Carry Advocates Association, Texas Rifle Association,* ...and this doesn't even scratch the surface. Without question, no organization has done as much politically as the National Rifle Association when it comes to protecting the rights of citizens to bear arms as well as promoting the shooting sports. It would be time and money well-invested to find an organization in your community that supports the shooting sports and is an advocate of our Second Amendment rights and join it.

To join The National Rifle Association, or to renew your membership, call 1-877-672-2000 today.

Firearm Manufacturers

Beretta USA Corp. – 17601 Beretta Drive – Accokeek, MD 20607   1-800-237-3882

Colt Manufacturing Co., LLC. - 547 New Park Ave, West Hartford, CT 06110   1 (800) 962-2658

Charter Arms, Inc. - 18 Brewster Lane, Shelton, Connecticut 06484   (866)-769-4867

CZ – USA, Inc., - P.O. Box 171073. Kansas City, KS
66117-0073   1-800-955-4486

Glock USA, Inc. - 6000 Highlands Parkway
Smyrna, GA 30082, U.S.A.   1- 770 - 432 1202

Kimber Manufacturing, Inc. - 30 Lower Valley Road
Kalispell, MT 59901 (888) 243-4522

Sig Sauer Inc. - 72 Pease Boulevard,
Newington, NH 03801   Phone: 603-610-3000

Sturm Ruger & Co., Inc. - 411 Sunapee Street.
Newport, NH 03773. (603) 865-2442

Smith & Wesson, Co., Inc. - 2100 Roosevelt Avenue
Springfield, MA 01104 (USA) 1-800-331-0852

Springfield Armory - 420 W Main St, Geneseo, IL 61254
(800) 617-6751.

Taurus USA, Inc. - 16175 NW 49 Avenue.
Miami Lakes, FL 33014   (305) 624-1115

Walther Arms, Inc. - 7700 Chad Colley Blvd
Fort Smith, AR 72916 (479) 242-8500

Rossi Firearms, Inc., - 16175 NW 49 Avenue
Miami Lakes, FL 33014 - (305) 474-0401

FN Herstal Arms Manufacturing Co., - PO Box 9424
McLean, VA 22102 – USA – 703–288 -3500

Heckler & Koch USA, - 5675 Transport Boulevard
Columbus, Georgia 31907 - (706) 568-1906

Reference Notes

1. As could be expected, nationwide average response time for a 911 call varies greatly from one area to another. For example, in Denver, Colorado, "...Priority 0-2 calls, response times increased from an average of 11.4 minutes to 14.3 minutes from 2008 to 2013. For Priority 3-6 calls, response times increased from an average of 20.5 minutes to 23.3 minutes."

2. Exclusive of those states and localities in which handguns are prohibited.

3. Bernhard Goetz is best known as the "*Subway Vigilante*" for shooting four teenagers during an attempted mugging in a New York City subway car in 1984.

4. Current as of January 1, 2017.

5. Patrick Sherrill committed the first in a series of tragic shootings at post offices in the United States.

6. James L. Buchanan, known affectionately by his family as "*Sonny Boy*," was the eleventh victim of the DC Sniper.

7. The Bersa Ultra Compact Pro in .45ACP.

8. Statistics published in 2014, 2015, 1nd 2016.

9. The questions posed on form 4473 are subject to frequent change.

10. It should be noted that the data base used to purge criminal history is a state comprised data base.

11. The practice of martial arts can sometimes prompt a criminal or assailant into the use of deadly force in order to subdue their victims.

12 Semi-automatic pistols equipped with a *'de-cocking'* feature can be fired immediately in a double-action mode without the necessity of cocking the hammer.

13 In some circumstances, brandishing is considered a felony which can result in the permanent loss of a citizen's right to own and carry firearms.

14 An amendment to the Omnibus Consolidated Appropriations Act of 1997, enacted by the 104th United States Congress in 1996, which bans access to firearms by people convicted of crimes of domestic violence. The act is often referred to as "the Lautenberg Amendment" after its sponsor, Senator Frank Lautenberg.

15 The Gun Control Act of 1968 (GCA or GCA68) is a U.S. federal law that regulates the firearms industry and firearms owners. It primarily focuses on regulating interstate commerce in firearms by generally prohibiting interstate firearms transfers except among licensed manufacturers, dealers and importers. The GCA was signed into law by President Lyndon B. Johnson on October 22, 1968, and is Title I of the U.S. federal firearms laws. The National Firearms Act of 1934 (NFA) is Title II. Both GCA and NFA are enforced by the Bureau of Alcohol, Tobacco, Firearms and Explosives (ATF).

16 *'Church Sexton'* is a custodian, or someone who is paid or non-paid to perform a janitorial service.

17 Dry firing some handguns can promote damage to the firing pin or the firing pin mechanism. Check with the manufacturer to see if dry-firing is permissible with your handgun, or purchase snap caps for your gun.

18   In addition to the NRA's lobby efforts for gun owner's, the National Rifle Association sponsors more than 50 national shooting championships each year and sanctions over 11,000 shooting tournaments.

19   The .40 S&W cartridge has been called the "ideal cartridge for personal defense and law enforcement."

20   The .40 S&W was specifically developed to duplicate performance of the FBI's reduced-velocity 10mm cartridge and fit into medium-frame (9mm size) automatic handguns. It debuted January 17, 1990, along with the new Smith and Wesson 4006 pistol.

Notes